FLORIDA

SCIENCE
FUSiON

fusion [FYOO • zhuhn] a mixture or blend formed by fusing two or more things

This Interactive Student Edition belongs to

_____

Teacher/Room

_____

HOUGHTON MIFFLIN HARCOURT

Consulting Authors

Michael A. DiSpezio
Global Educator
North Falmouth, Massachusetts

Marjorie Frank
Science Writer and Content-Area Reading Specialist
Brooklyn, New York

Michael Heithaus
Director, School of Environment and Society
Associate Professor, Department of Biological Sciences
Florida International University
North Miami, Florida

Donna Ogle
Professor of Reading and Language
National-Louis University
Chicago, Illinois

 HOUGHTON MIFFLIN HARCOURT

Front Cover: *sea turtle* © Westend6l GmbH/Alamy; *water bubbles* © Andrew Holt/Alamy; *guitar and saxophone* © Brand Z/Alamy; *giraffe* © The Africa Image Library/Alamy; *observatory* © Robert Llewellyn/Workbook Stock/Getty Images; *wind turbines* © Comstock/Getty Images.

Back Cover: *ferns* © Mauro Fermariello/Photo Researchers, Inc.; *galaxy* © Stocktrek/Corbis; *clownfish* © Georgette Douwma/Photographer's Choice/Getty Images; *prism* © Larry Lilac/Alamy

Program Advisors

Paul D. Asimow
*Professor of Geology and
    Geochemistry*
California Institute of Technology
Pasadena, California

Bobby Jeanpierre
*Associate Professor of Science
    Education*
University of Central Florida
Orlando, Florida

Gerald H. Krockover
*Professor of Earth and Atmospheric
    Science Education*
Purdue University
West Lafayette, Indiana

Rose Pringle
*Associate Professor
    School of Teaching and Learning*
College of Education
University of Florida
Gainesville, Florida

Carolyn Staudt
Curriculum Designer for Technology
KidSolve, Inc.
The Concord Consortium
Concord, Massachusetts

Larry Stookey
Science Department
Antigo High School
Antigo, Wisconsin

Carol J. Valenta
*Senior Vice President and Associate
    Director of the Museum*
Saint Louis Science Center
St. Louis, Missouri

Barry A. Van Deman
President and CEO
Museum of Life and Science
Durham, North Carolina

Florida Reviewers

Janet M. Acerra
Forest Lakes Elementary
Oldsmar, Florida

Shannan Combee
Inwood Elementary
Winter Haven, Florida

Amber J. Cooley
Jacksonville Heights Elementary
Jacksonville, Florida

Donna de la Paz
Trinity Oaks Elementary
New Port Richey, Florida

Nancy Carrier Duncan
Eustis Heights Elementary
Eustis, Florida

Marsha Dwyer
Kenwood K-8 Center
Miami, Florida

Jessica S. Fowler
Susie E. Tolbert Elementary
Jacksonville, Florida

Pat Houston
Northwood Elementary
Crestview, Florida

Timothy W. Peterson
Romeo Elementary
Dunnellon, Florida

Rosanne Phillips
Kenwood K-8 Center
Miami, Florida

Rose M. Sedely
Eustis Heights Elementary
Eustis, Florida

Gerilyn Stark-Jerry
Chain of Lakes Elementary
Winter Haven, Florida

Deborah S. Street
Southport Elementary
Southport, Florida

Janine Townsley
Norwood Elementary
Miami, Florida

Jessica Weiss
Westchase Elementary
Tampa, Florida

Power up with Science Fusion!

Your program fuses. . .

Online Virtual Experiences

Hands-on Explorations

Active Reading

. . .to generate science energy for you.

Active Reading

Be an active reader and make this book your own!

Write your ideas, answer questions, make notes, and record activity results right on these pages.

Your book will become a record of everything you learn in science.

Hands-on Explorations

Science is all about doing.

Ask questions and test your ideas.

Draw conclusions and share what you learn.

Do the exciting activities on the Inquiry Flipchart.

How Does the Sun Warm Our Homes?

How does solar energy warm our homes? Make a model to find out.

Materials

cardboard box   tape

scissors   2 thermometers

plastic wrap

1. Use the box and the plastic wrap to make a model house. **Caution!** Be careful when using scissors.

2. Tape one thermometer into a window of the house. Record the temperatures on both thermometers.

3. Put the house in a sunny spot. Lay the other thermometer next to the house. Wait 1 hour. Record both temperatures again. Compare the numbers.

Online Virtual Experiences

Use a computer to make science come alive.

Explore cool labs and activities in the virtual world.

Science Fusion
is new energy just for YOU!

Contents

Track Your Progress

EARTH AND SPACE SCIENCE

Unit 3—Weather

Big Idea 7

Earth Systems and Patterns

Big Idea 8

Properties of Matter

PHYSICAL SCIENCE

PHYSICAL SCIENCE

Unit 7—Forces and Motion............ 161

Big Idea 8

Properties of Matter

Big Idea 13

Forces and Changes in Motion

LIFE SCIENCE

Unit 8—The Human Body................ 191

Big Idea 14

Organization and Development of Living Organisms

LIFE SCIENCE

Work Like a Scientist

Big Idea 1

The Practice of Science

Thomas Edison's lab in
Fort Myers, Florida

I Wonder Why

Scientists use tools to find out about things. Why?
Turn the page to find out.

Here's Why Tools help scientists learn more than they could with just their senses.

Essential Questions and Florida Benchmarks

Big Idea 1 *Scientists ask questions about the world around them. They find answers by investigating through a variety of methods.*

Now I Get the Big Idea!

SC.2.N.1.1 Raise questions . . . investigate them in teams . . . and generate appropriate explanations based on those explorations. **SC.2.N.1.3** Ask "how do you know?" in appropriate situations . . . . **SC.2.N.1.5** Distinguish between empirical observation . . . and ideas or inferences . . . .

Essential Question

How Do We Use Inquiry Skills?

Engage Your Brain!

Find the answer in this lesson.

You tell how these flowers are alike and different.

You are

_____ them.

Active Reading

Lesson Vocabulary

1 Preview the lesson.

2 Write the vocabulary term here.

_____

Use Inquiry Skills

Inquiry skills help people find out information. Inquiry skills help people plan and do tests.

These children use inquiry skills to do a task for school. They are observing. Observe means to use your five senses to learn about things.

What can we observe in my backyard?

4

Danny and Sophie want to observe things in the backyard. They plan an investigation. They plan how to find out what they want to know. They also predict, or make a good guess, about what they will observe.

► This page names three inquiry skills. Circle the name for one of the skills.

Explore the Backyard

Danny and Sophie head out to the backyard to begin their task. Danny finds the length and the height of the birdhouse. He measures it with a ruler.

Active Reading

Find the sentence that explains what it means to **measure**. Draw a line under the sentence.

They use inquiry skills to learn more about the backyard.

Sophie compares leaves. She observes how they are alike and how they are different. She may also classify, or sort, many leaves in the backyard by the way they are alike.

▶ Look at Sophie's leaves. Put them in order of size from smallest to largest.

_____ _____ _____

Model and Infer

Now Danny and Sophie draw a map of the backyard. They are making a model to show what something is like. You could also make a model to show how something works.

My Backyard

birch tree

rose bush

maple tree

bird bath

bird house

Active Reading

Find the sentences that explain what it means to **make a model**. Draw a line under the sentences.

Danny and Sophie use one more inquiry skill. They infer. They use what they know to answer a question—Are there any living things in the backyard? They can infer that the backyard is home to many plants and animals.

▶ Think about what you know about winter. Infer what Danny and Sophie might observe in the backyard during winter.

_____

_____

Sum It Up!

① Complete It!

Fill in the blank.

How are measuring, observing, and predicting alike?

They are all

_____ .

② Circle It!

Circle the skill name to match the meaning.

Which one means to choose steps you will do to learn something?

infer

plan an investigation

classify

③ Draw and Write It!

Observe something outside. Then draw and write to record your observations.

_____

_____

Brain Check

Name _____

Word Play

Read each clue below. Then unscramble the letters to write the correct answer.

| observe | compare | measure | infer |

1 to find the size or amount of something

s e m a r e u _____

2 to use your senses to learn about something

b o s r e e v _____

3 to observe how things are alike and different

p o c r a m e _____

4 to use what you know to answer a question

f n i r e _____

Apply Concepts

Match each inquiry skill to its meaning.

to make a good guess about what will happen	plan an investigation
to sort things by how they are alike	classify
to show what something is like or how it works	predict
to follow steps to answer a question	make a model

Take It Home!

Family Members: Work with your child to measure two objects in your home. Have your child compare the two objects and tell which is larger.

SC.2.N.1.2 Compare the observations made by different groups using the same tools.

Essential Question

How Do We Use Science Tools?

Find the answer to the question in the lesson.

What does a thermometer measure?

_____

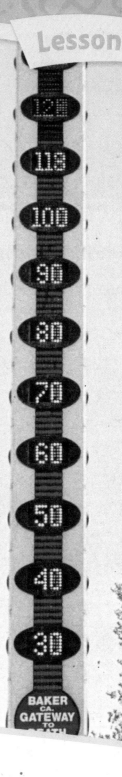

Active Reading

Lesson Vocabulary

1 Preview the lesson.

2 Write the 2 vocabulary terms here.

_____   _____

Top Tools

You use tools every day. Tools are things that help you do a job. **Science tools** help you find out information.

A hand lens is one science tool. It helps you observe more details than with your eyes alone.

▶ What can you see through this hand lens? Circle it.

A hand lens makes things look larger.

Measuring Tools

You use some tools for measuring things. You use a **thermometer** to measure temperature. You use a measuring cup to measure amounts of liquids.

Active Reading

The main idea is the most important idea about something. Draw a line under the main idea on this page.

A thermometer measures temperature in units called degrees.

A measuring cup measures liquids in units called milliliters, cups, and ounces.

Measure More!

You use a tool called a scale to measure weight. You can use a balance to measure mass.

This scale measures weight in units called pounds and ounces.

▶ Name two things you can weigh on a scale.

_____

_____

This balance measures mass in units called grams and kilograms.

You use a ruler and a tape measure to measure distance as well as length, width, and height. Both tools measure in units called inches or centimeters.

▶ Circle the object the ruler is measuring.

A ruler measures objects with straight lines.

A tape measure can measure around an object.

17

Sum It Up!

① Answer It!

Write the answer to this question.

You want to measure how much water fits into a pail. What tool could you use?

_____

② Draw It!

Draw yourself using a measuring tool.

③ Mark It!

Mark an X on the tool that does _not_ measure.

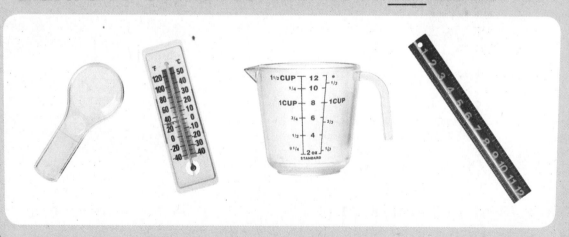

18

Brain Check

Lesson 2

Name ______________________

Word Play

Match the name of each tool to its picture.

tape measure	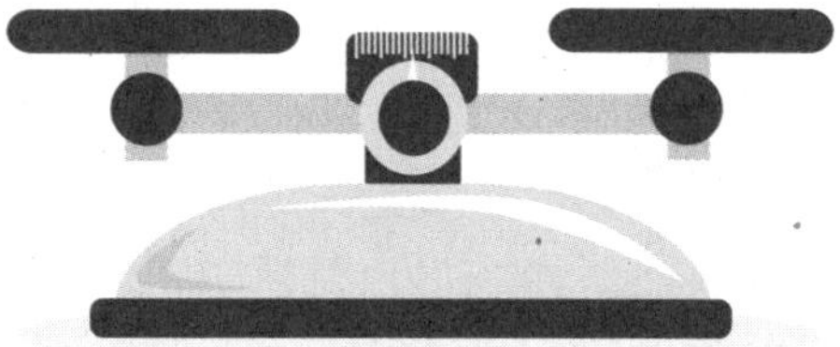
balance	
thermometer	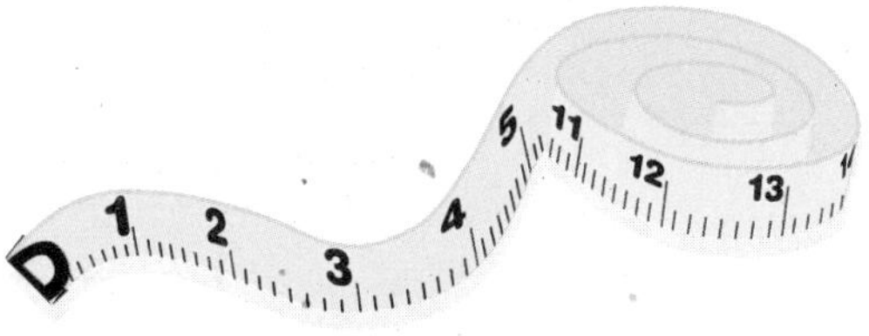
measuring cup	
hand lens	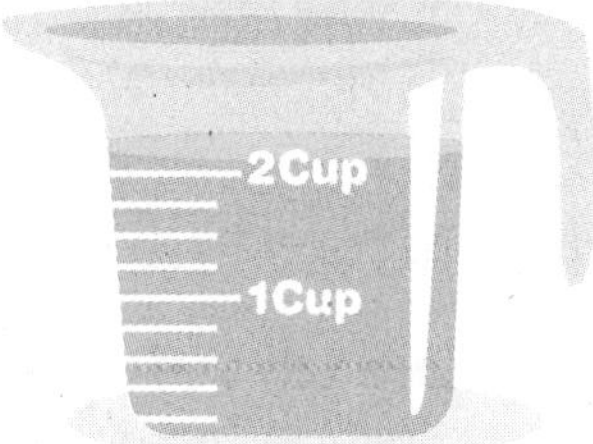

Name the tool you could use for each job.

measuring the length of a book	_____
finding the weight of a watermelon	_____
observing curves and lines on the tip of your finger	_____

Take It Home!

Family Members: Go on a scavenger hunt. See which tools from this lesson you have in or around your home. Discuss with your child how to use each tool.

1

In 1742, Celsius invented the Celsius scale to measure temperature.

2

The temperature at which water freezes on the Celsius scale is 0°.

4

Things to Know About

Anders Celsius

3

The temperature at which water boils on the Celsius scale is 100°.

4

Celsius was an astronomer, or a person who studies the stars and other things in space.

Celsius Match Up

1

▶ Read each thermometer. Write the number that matches the correct temperature in each picture.

2

3

▶ How does a temperature scale help you tell about the weather?

_____

_____

SC.2.N.1.1 Raise questions about the natural world, investigate them in teams through free exploration and systematic observations, and generate appropriate explanations based on those explorations. **SC.2.N.1.2** Compare the observations made by different groups using the same tools.

Name _____

Essential Question

What Tools Can We Use?

Set a Purpose

Write what you want to find out.

_____

_____

Think About the Procedure

1 Which science tool did you choose? What does it do?

_____

_____

2 How will the tool help you observe the object?

_____

_____

Record Your Data

Record your observations in this chart.

My Object _____	
My Tool _____	
What I Learned Without the Tool	What I Learned With the Tool

Draw Conclusions

How can a science tool help you learn more about an object?

_____

_____

_____

Ask More Questions

What other questions can you ask about how science tools are used?

_____

_____

_____

SC.2.N.1.1 Raise questions . . . investigate them . . . and generate appropriate explanations based on those explorations. SC.2.N.1.3 Ask "how do you know?" in appropriate situations . . . . SC.2.N.1.4 Explain how . . . scientific investigations should yield similar conclusions . . . . SC.2.N.1.5 Distinguish between empirical observation . . . and ideas or inferences . . . .

Lesson 4

Essential Question

How Do Scientists Think?

Engage Your Brain!

Find the answer in the lesson.

When scientists

_____

they follow steps and use tools to answer a question.

Active Reading

Lesson Vocabulary

1 Preview the lesson.

2 Write the 4 vocabulary terms here.

_____   _____

_____   _____

Let's Observe It!

Scientists **investigate**. They plan and do a test to answer a question or solve a problem. They use inquiry skills and science tools to help them.

There are many ways to investigate. But many scientists follow a sequence, or order of events. Here's one possible sequence. First, scientists may observe and ask a question.

Active Reading

Clue words can help you find the order of things. **First** is a clue word. Circle this clue word in the paragraph above.

Does food coloring spread faster in cold water or warm water?

cold

Now, scientists can make a hypothesis. A **hypothesis** is a statement that can be tested. Then scientists plan a fair test. The scientists list the materials they will need and the steps they will take to do their test.

Food coloring spreads faster in warm water.

food coloring

warm

Let's Test It!

Next, the scientists are ready to do their test. They follow their plan and record what they observe.

Active Reading

Clue words can help you find the order of things. **Next** is a clue word. Circle this clue word in the paragraph above.

These children test whether food coloring spreads faster in cold water or warm water.

After the test, scientists **draw conclusions**. They use the information they have gathered to decide if their results support the hypothesis. Finally, they write or draw to **communicate** what they learned.

▶ How does the temperature of water affect how fast the food coloring spreads? Draw a conclusion.

_____

_____

_____

▶ What else could a scientist test with water and food coloring?

_____

_____

_____

warm

Let's Check Again!

Scientists do the same test a few times. They need to make sure that they get similar results every time. In this investigation, the food coloring should spread faster in warm water every time.

Our Food Colori

cold   warm   cold   warm

Monday   Wednesday

► Look at the **warm** cup for both Monday and Friday. Draw a conclusion. Color in the **warm** cup for Wednesday to show what it should look like.

Test

cold   warm

Friday

Do the Math!

Measure Length

Choose an object. Use a ruler to measure the object's length. Measure it three times. Record.

Length of _____	
Measure 1	
Measure 2	
Measure 3	

1. How do your numbers compare?

_____

_____

2. Why do you think so?

_____

_____

_____

Sum It Up!

1 Order It!

Number the steps from 1 to 4 to tell a way scientists investigate.

_____ Observe and ask a question.

_____ Do the test and record what happens.

_____ Draw conclusions and communicate.

_____ Make a hypothesis and plan a fair test.

2 Circle It!

Circle the correct answer.

Suppose you make a poster to show the results of your test. You are _____.

observing   planning your test

making a hypothesis   communicating

Brain Check

Lesson 4

Name _____

Word Play

Circle the word to complete each sentence.

1. You use inquiry skills and science tools to learn. You _____.

   communicate   investigate

2. You take the first step to do an investigation. You _____.

   draw conclusions   observe

3. You make a statement that you can test. You make a _____.

   hypothesis   conclusion

4. You use information you gathered to explain what you learned. You _____.

   draw conclusions   observe

5. You write to tell about the results of a test. You _____.

   communicate   ask a question

© Houghton Mifflin Harcourt Publishing Company

33

Apply Concepts

These steps show a test some children did.
Label each box with a step from this lesson.

The children look at an ice cube. They ask—
Will it melt in the sun?

Observe and _____.

↓

They form a statement that the ice cube will melt
in the sun.

_____.

↓

They follow their plan. The ice cube melts! They
decide that the sun's heat caused the ice to melt.

Test and _____.

↓

The children write and draw to tell the results
of their test.

_____.

Take It Home!

Family Members: Work with your child to plan an
investigation. Use the steps from this lesson.

SC.2.N.1.1 Raise questions about the natural world, investigate them in teams through free exploration and systematic observations, and generate appropriate explanations based on those explorations. **SC.2.N.1.6** Explain how scientists alone or in groups are always investigating new ways to solve problems.

Name _____

Essential Question

How Do We Solve a Problem?

Set a Purpose

What problem do you want to solve?

_____

_____

Think About the Procedure

1 Why do you make a list of the properties the holder must have?

_____

_____

2 Why do you design your holder before you build it?

_____

_____

Record Your Data

Record the details of your plan in this chart.

The Problem
My Plan
Materials I need

Draw Conclusions

Sometimes it is helpful to make a model first before making the real thing. How can making a model help you solve a problem?

_____

_____

Ask More Questions

What other questions do you have about designing and making models to solve problems?

_____

_____

Name _____

Multiple Choice

Fill in the circle next to the best answer.

SC.2.N.1.3

1 Jared knows that his two blocks are the same color but different shapes. How does he know?

(A) He measures them.

(B) He observes and compares them.

(C) He makes a model.

SC.2.N.1.1

2 Gail uses this tool to find the length of a book.

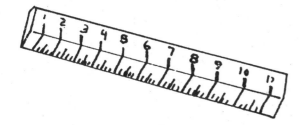

What is she doing?

(A) classifying

(B) inferring

(C) measuring

SC.2.N.1.2

3 Victor uses a scale to measure the weight of a melon. He observes that the melon weighs three pounds. Ana also uses a scale to measure the weight of the same melon. What should Ana observe?

(A) The melon weighs two pounds.

(B) The melon weighs three pounds.

(C) The melon weighs four pounds.

SC.2.N.1.4

4 Lea investigates to answer a question. Then she repeats her experiment several times. Which will **most likely** be true?

(A) The results will be the same.

(B) The results will be different.

(C) She cannot compare the results.

SC.2.N.1.5

5 Sumeet looks at the sky before he goes to school. It is dark and cloudy outside. What skill is Sumeet using?

(A) compare

(B) infer

(C) observe

SC.2.N.1.6

6 How do scientists work to solve problems?

(A) They solve problems the same way each time.

(B) They always work alone.

(C) They keep looking for new ways to solve problems.

Earth's Surface

Big Idea 6

Earth Structures

Fort Jefferson, Florida Keys

I Wonder Why

People use materials from Earth to build things. Why?
Turn the page to find out.

Here's Why Earth materials such as rock are easy to find. They also last a long time and are strong enough to build structures.

Big Idea 6 *Humans continue to explore Earth's surface. Humans need Earth resources like rocks and soil.*

Now I Get the Big Idea!

© Houghton Mifflin Harcourt Publishing Company

SC.2.E.6.1 Recognize that Earth is made up of rocks. Rocks come in many sizes and shapes.

Essential Question

What Are Rocks?

Engage Your Brain!

Find the answer to the question in the lesson.

Where can you find rocks?

Rocks are all

over _____ .

Active Reading

Lesson Vocabulary

1 Preview the lesson.

2 Write the 2 vocabulary terms here.

_____   _____

Rocks Rock!

Earth is made up of rock. A **rock** is a hard, nonliving object from the ground. Rocks can be different sizes. A boulder is a very large rock. A pebble is a very small rock. Sand is made of many tiny pieces of rock.

boulder

sand

▶ Name a size of rock you see on this page.

_____

Weathering changes big rocks into smaller rocks. **Weathering** is what happens when wind and water break down rock into smaller pieces.

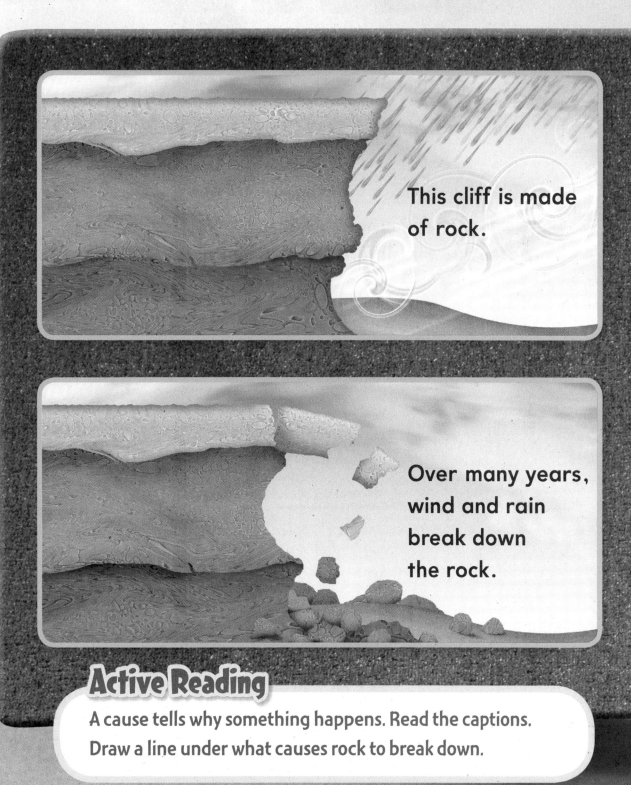

This cliff is made of rock.

Over many years, wind and rain break down the rock.

Active Reading

A cause tells why something happens. Read the captions. Draw a line under what causes rock to break down.

Great Rock Groups

Rocks are made up of minerals. All rocks do not look and feel the same. They have different minerals and form in different ways.

Active Reading

Clue words can help you find ways things are different. Draw a box around the clue word **different** each time you see it on this page.

Size
Rocks can be different sizes.

Shape

Rocks can be different shapes.

▶ Write another way you might group rocks.

_____

_____

Color

Rocks can be different colors, too.

Rock Resources

People use rocks every day. We use rocks to build things like walls and homes. We use rocks to make art. Rocks are very helpful!

This home and wall are made of rock.

This sculpture is made of rock.

Read the word problem. Answer the questions.

Mike observes a brown rock and a gray rock in his yard. The brown rock weighs 11 pounds. The gray rock weighs 13 pounds.

1. Use > and < to compare the weights of the rocks.

   _____ > _____

   _____ < _____

2. Which rock is heavier?

   the _____ rock

▶ Draw one way people use rocks.

Sum It Up!

① Draw It!

Draw each rock. Then write how the rocks are different.

pebble

_____

_____

boulder

_____

_____

② Write It!

Where can you see rocks around your home? Explain.

_____

_____

③ Circle It!

Circle the sentence that is true.

Rocks are made up of minerals.

Rocks have the same shape.

Name _____

Word Play

Fill in the blanks. Use each word from
the word bank.

| rock | pebbles | sand | weathering |

The next time you see a big _____,
look closely. Someday the rock may be much smaller!
Wind and rain may wear away at the rock. This is
called _____. Over time, the rock may
break down into small _____. Perhaps
the pebbles will someday break down into tiny pieces
of _____.

You rock!

Fill in the chart. Show how rocks can be alike and different.

Rocks

Alike	Different
made of minerals	size

Family Members: Work with your child to identify objects made from rocks in and around your home.

© Houghton Mifflin Harcourt Publishing Company

SC.2.N.1.6 Explain how scientists alone or in groups are always investigating new ways to solve problems. SC.2.E.6.1 Recognize that Earth is made up of rocks. Rocks come in many sizes and shapes.

People in Science

Learn About...

Dr. Florence Bascom

Dr. Florence Bascom was a geologist, or a person who studies rocks. She began her work in the 1890s. At that time, most women did not study science. Dr. Bascom wanted other women to learn about rocks, so she taught geology at a women's college. She also traveled to the Grand Canyon and other places to study rocks.

Fun Fact

Bascom used tools like these to study rocks.

51

Know Your Rocks

Dr. Florence Bascom studied rocks. Here's your chance!

▶ Write the number of each description next to the correct rock.

(____) quartz

1 This white rock is used for statues and building materials.

2 This white crystal is a mineral. It is found in many places.

(____) sandstone

3 This shiny black rock is called volcanic glass. It was formed from lava from a volcano.

(____) pumice

4 This brown rock is made of tiny grains.

5 This rock has air holes and may float in water.

(____) marble

(____) obsidian

SC.2.E.6.2 Describe how small pieces of rock and dead plant and animal parts can be the basis of soil and explain the process by which soil is formed. SC.2.E.6.3 Classify soil types based on color, texture (size of particles), the ability to retain water, and the ability to support the growth of plants.

Essential Question

What Is Soil?

Engage Your Brain!

Find the answer to the question in the lesson.

How can people use soil?

to _____

Active Reading

Lesson Vocabulary

1 Preview the lesson.

2 Write the 4 vocabulary terms here.

_____   _____

_____   _____

Super Soil

Soil is made up of small pieces of rock and once-living things. We use soil to grow plants.

Active Reading

Find the sentence that tells the meaning of **soil**. Draw a line under the sentence.

Soil forms a layer on parts of Earth's surface.

Soil forms when weathering breaks down rock. The small pieces of rock form the base of soil. At the same time, dead plants and animals fall to the ground. These once-living things break down into bits. The bits become part of soil, too.

Soil is made of many tiny pieces mixed together.

▶ What can you observe about this soil?

_____

_____

It Takes All Kinds

There are many kinds of soil. Soils can be different colors. Some soils can hold more water than other soils. Some soils are better for growing plants. Sand, humus, and clay are some of the things found in soil. Different amounts of these things make kinds of soil different.

Some soil gets very hard when it is dry. The soil in this desert does not hold water well or grow many plants.

Sand is made up of tiny pieces of rock. Sandy soil does not hold water well. Many plants cannot grow in it.

Humus is made of once-living things. Soil that has a lot of humus holds water well and is good for growing many kinds of plants.

Clay is sticky when wet and smooth when dry. Soil that has a lot of clay holds water well but many plants do not grow well in it.

▶ Circle the picture of the part of soil that helps many kinds of plants grow.

Sum It Up!

① Write It!

Write two things that soil is made of.

_____

_____

② Order It!

Write 1, 2, 3 to show the order of how a plant becomes part of soil.

___ The plant begins to break into pieces.

___ A plant dies and falls to the ground.

___ The pieces get smaller and become part of soil.

③ Draw It!

Draw a picture of humus and a picture of sand.

Name _____

Word Play

Match each part of soil to its description.
Then add another fact about it.

sand

humus

clay

It is sticky when it is wet.

_____

_____

It has tiny pieces of rock you
can see with your eyes alone.

_____

_____

It can hold water well.

_____

_____

Dig it!

Apply Concepts

Fill in the chart. Show how soil forms.

How Soil Forms

```
┌─────────────────────────────────────────┐
│                                          │
│  _____ │
│                                          │
│  _____ │
│                                          │
│  _____ │
└─────────────────────────────────────────┘
                     │
                     ▼
┌─────────────────────────────────────────┐
│                                          │
│  _____ │
│                                          │
│  _____ │
│                                          │
│  _____ │
└─────────────────────────────────────────┘
                     │
                     ▼
┌─────────────────────────────────────────┐
│   All the bits mix together to make soil.│
└─────────────────────────────────────────┘
```

Take It Home!

Family Members: Walk with your child near your home to observe soil in your area. Have your child name some properties of the soil.

SC.2.N.1.1 Raise questions . . . investigate them in teams . . . and generate appropriate explanations based on those explorations. **SC.2.N.1.3** Ask "how do you know?" in appropriate situations . . . **SC.2.N.1.5** Distinguish between empirical observation . . . and ideas or inferences . . . **SC.2.E.6.3** Classify soil types based on . . . the ability to support the growth of plants.

Name _____

Essential Question
How Do Soils Differ?

Set a Purpose
Write what you want to find out.

_____

Make a Prediction
Predict what you think will happen.

_____

_____

Think About the Procedure
How will you test the soils?

_____

_____

_____

Record Your Data

In this chart, record what you observe.

	What does the soil look like?	What happened to the seed after one week?
Soil #1		
Soil #2		
Soil #3		

Draw Conclusions

Which kind of soil was best for growing plants? How do you know?

_____

_____

_____

Ask More Questions

What other questions could you ask about soil?

_____

_____

Name _____

Multiple Choice

Fill in the circle next to the best answer.

SC.2.E.6.1

1 Which is smallest?

Ⓐ a boulder

Ⓑ a pebble

Ⓒ a piece of sand

SC.2.E.6.1

2 How are these rocks sorted?

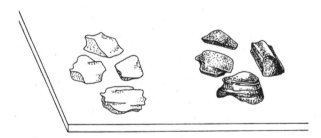

Ⓐ by color

Ⓑ by shape

Ⓒ by size

SC.2.E.6.2

3 What makes up soil?

Ⓐ only once-living things

Ⓑ only rocks and water

Ⓒ rocks and once-living things

SC.2.N.1.3, SC.2.N.1.5, SC.2.E.6.3

4 Desmond knows that soils with different textures are made of different materials. How does he know?

Ⓐ He places the soils in boxes.

Ⓑ He observes the soils carefully.

Ⓒ He plants a shrub in one of the soils.

SC.2.E.6.3

5 Jill observes the size of the grains in this soil. Which tool does she use?

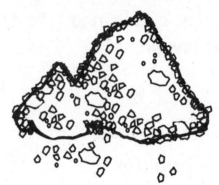

Ⓐ a balance

Ⓑ a hand lens

Ⓒ a thermometer

UNIT 3
Weather

Big Idea 7

Earth Systems and Patterns

Big Idea 8

Properties of Matter

hurricanes over Florida

I Wonder Why

People keep extra food and other things in case of a storm. Why?
Turn the page to find out.

Here's Why People keep extra things in case the power goes out and stores are closed.

Track Your Progress

Essential Questions and Florida Benchmarks

Big Idea 7 *Weather changes from day to day and from season to season.*

Big Idea 8 *You can measure and compare the temperatures of things.*

Now I Get the Big Idea!

SC.2.E.7.1 Compare and describe changing patterns in nature that repeat themselves, such as weather conditions . . . day to day and season to season. **SC.2.E.7.4** Investigate that air is all around us and that moving air is wind. **SC.2.P.8.1** Observe and measure objects in terms of their properties, including . . . temperature . . . .

Essential Question

How Does Weather Change?

Engage Your Brain!

Find the answer to the question in the lesson.

When might you see ice on plants?

You might see this in _____.

Active Reading

Lesson Vocabulary

1 Preview the lesson.

2 Write the 6 vocabulary terms here.

_____   _____

_____   _____

_____   _____

Wonderful Weather

Weather is what the air outside is like. Weather may be sunny, rainy, cloudy, snowy, or windy. It can be hot or cold outside. Weather can change quickly or it can change over many days or months. A weather change that repeats is called a weather pattern.

Active Reading

The main idea is the most important idea about something. Draw a line under the main idea on this page.

You may see thin or puffy clouds on a sunny day. Low, gray clouds usually bring rain.

Clouds help predict weather.

On some days, rain falls.

▶ Draw what the weather is like today.

In some places, the weather gets very cold. Snow may fall.

Measure It!

You can use tools to measure weather.

A rain gauge measures precipitation.

Precipitation is water that falls from the sky.

Rain, snow, sleet, and hail are precipitation.

A thermometer measures temperature.

Temperature is how hot or cold something is.

Active Reading

Find the sentence that tells the meaning of **precipitation**. Draw a line under it.

Air is all around us. Wind is moving air. A weather vane tells the direction of the wind.

This thermometer measures temperature in degrees Fahrenheit and Celsius.

A rain gauge tells how much rain falls.

Do the Math!

Measure Temperature

Use a thermometer to measure the temperature of the air in the morning and in the afternoon. Color the pictures below to show the temperatures. Write the temperatures on the lines.

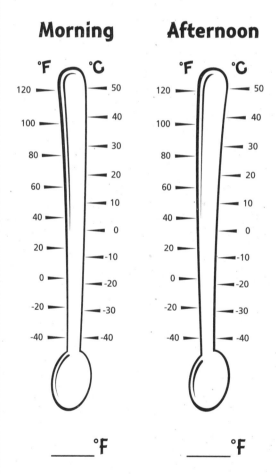

Morning

°F   °C

_____°F

Afternoon

°F   °C

_____°F

Write a subtraction sentence to find out how the temperature changed.

_____

Where Does the Water Go?

The **water cycle** is the way water moves from Earth's surface into the air and back again. The water cycle is a pattern. The water cycle causes weather to change.

The sun's heat makes water **evaporate**, or change to a gas. The gas is pushed up and meets cooler air.

▶ Where will the water go when the sun heats it?

_____

_____

_____

Then the gas cools and **condenses**, or changes into tiny drops of water. The drops form clouds.

Active Reading

A cause tells why something happens. What causes water drops to fall as rain or snow? Draw one line under the cause.

The water drops join to make bigger ones. The drops fall as precipitation.

The precipitation flows into rivers, lakes, and oceans. Then the water cycle starts again.

73

Season to Season

A season is a time of year that has a certain kind of weather. Weather changes each season. The seasons always follow the same pattern.

Fabulous Fall

In fall the air outside may be cool. The leaves of some trees change color and drop off.

Wonderful Winter

Winter is the coldest season. Ice can form on land and plants. In some places snow may fall. Winter has the fewest hours of daylight.

▶ Draw an activity you would do during summer.

Sunny Spring

In spring the air gets warmer. Some places get a lot of rain.

Super Summer

Summer is the warmest season. Some places have sudden storms. Summer has the most hours of daylight.

Sum It Up!

① Draw It!

Draw your favorite kind of weather.

② Match It!

Match each tool to what it measures.

temperature

rain

③ Complete It!

Fill in the blank.

The movement of water from Earth's surface into the air and back again is called the

_____ .

④ Order It!

Number the seasons to show their order. Start with winter.

___1___ winter

_____ summer

_____ fall

_____ spring

Name _____

Word Play

Read the clues. Use the words to complete the puzzle.

weather   temperature   precipitation   evaporate   condense

Across

1. The sun's heat can cause water to _____.

2. What the air outside is like is called _____.

3. Water can _____ into tiny drops.

Down

4. Water that falls as rain or snow is _____.

5. Use a thermometer to measure _____.

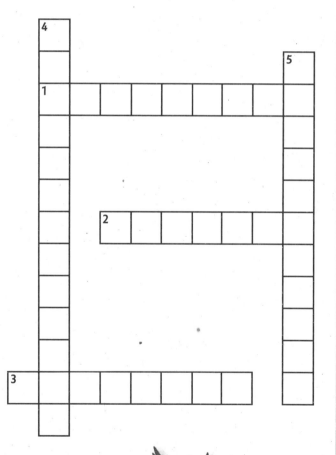

Apply Concepts

Fill in the chart. Show causes and effects in the water cycle.

The Water Cycle

Cause		Effect
The sun heats water on Earth's surface.	→	_____ _____ _____
Water condenses into drops.	→	_____ _____ _____
_____ _____ _____	→	The drops fall to Earth as rain or snow.

Take It Home!

Family Members: Watch or read a daily weather forecast with your child. Talk about why it can be helpful to predict weather.

© Houghton Mifflin Harcourt Publishing Company

Lesson

INQUIRY 2

SC.2.N.1.1 Raise questions . . .
investigate them in teams . . . and
generate appropriate explanations based
on those explorations. SC.2.N.1.2 Compare the
observations made by . . . using the same tools.
SC.2.N.1.3 Ask "how do you know?" in
appropriate situations . . . .
SC.2.E.7.2 Investigate . . . that the Sun's
energy . . . warms the water, land, and air.
SC.2.P.8.1 Observe and measure objects in
terms of their properties, ...

Name _____

Essential Question

How Does the Sun Heat Earth?

Set a Purpose

Write what you want to find out.

We Want to Find out What
happens To tempature oster it is
in The Sun

State Your Hypothesis

Write your hypothesis, or the statement that you will test.

I Think the tempadure will

_____

Think About the Procedure

How will you use the thermometers?

First,

_____

_____

Record Your Data

In this chart, record what you observe.

	Starting Temperature	Ending Temperature
air	70°	91°
water	71°	89°
soil	72°	104°

Draw Conclusions

How does the sun heat Earth's land, air, and water differently? How do you know?

Earth heats the soil the most. I know this because.

Ask More Questions

What other questions can you ask about the sun's heat?

Puede ser el calor o el frio

Name _____

SC.2.N.1.1 Raise questions . . . investigate them in teams . . . and generate appropriate explanations based on those explorations. **SC.2.N.1.2** Compare the observations made by . . . using the same tools. **SC.2.N.1.3** Ask "how do you know?" in appropriate situations . . . . **SC.2.N.1.4** Explain how scientific investigations should yield similar conclusions ___ **SC.2.E.7.3** Investigate, observe ___ water left in an open container disappears ___ water in a closed container does not disappear (evaporate).

Essential Question
What Is Evaporation?

Set a Purpose
Write what you want to find out.

_____

_____

State Your Hypothesis
Write your hypothesis, or the statement that you will test.

_____

Think About the Procedure

1 Why should both containers start with the same amount of water?

_____

2 Why does one container have a lid?

_____

_____

Record Your Data

In this chart, record what you observe.

	How much water?	
	Before	After
Container with a Lid		
Container with no Lid		

Draw Conclusions

What happened to the water in the open container?
How do you know?

_____

_____

Ask More Questions

What other questions can you ask about evaporation?

_____

_____

SC.2.E.7.5 State the importance of preparing for severe weather, lightning, and other weather related events.

Essential Question

How Can We Prepare for Severe Weather?

🧠 Engage Your Brain!

Find the answer to the question in the lesson.

When can wind take the shape of a cone?

when there is a

_____

Active Reading

Lesson Vocabulary

1 Preview the lesson.

2 Write the 4 vocabulary terms here.

_____ _____

_____ _____

Wild Weather

Sometimes weather gets wild! Then we have severe, or very bad, weather. A thunderstorm is one kind of severe weather. A **thunderstorm** is a storm with a lot of rain, thunder, and lightning.

Active Reading

A detail is a fact about a main idea. Draw one line under a detail. Draw an arrow to the main idea it tells about.

Lightning is a flash of electricity in the sky.

A tornado is a kind of severe weather, too. A **tornado** is a spinning cloud with a cone shape. A tornado has very strong winds.

Another kind of severe weather is a hurricane. A **hurricane** is a large storm with heavy rain and strong winds.

▶ What weather does this picture show? Label it.

_____

A hurricane can cause a lot of damage to an area.

Safety First

Storms can be dangerous. Scientists called meteorologists predict storms. They warn people about storms. Then people can do things to stay safe and be prepared for storms.

Meteorologists use tools such as computers to help predict and track severe weather.

▶ What might happen if meteorologists couldn't predict weather in your area?

_____

_____

Tips for Storm Safety

Read these tips on how to get ready for a storm. Then add your own tip at the bottom.

1. Get extra food and water.

2. Get other things you may need, such as flashlights and blankets.

3. Make a plan for your family and pets.

4. Stay inside.

5. _____

_____

_____

People try to protect property from severe weather.

Sum It Up!

① Solve It!

Fill in the blank.

What kind of storm

is made up of

and  ?

_____

② Draw It!

Draw yourself preparing for severe weather.

③ Circle It!

Circle the pictures that show severe weather.

Word Play

Find each word in the puzzle. Then answer the questions.

| thunderstorm | hurricane | lightning | tornado |

```
q  i  g  g  d  o  r  a  s  t  i  e
t  h  u  n  d  e  r  s  t  o  r  m
l  s  j  k  d  a  z  y  l  r  p  a
e  v  h  u  r  r  i  c  a  n  e  m
w  a  t  r  s  p  l  i  t  a  r  f
b  w  e  g  l  n  o  w  t  d  u  i
l  i  g  h  t  n  i  n  g  o  r  b
```

1 What might you see during a thunderstorm?

_____

2 What kind of storm always has heavy rain and strong winds?

_____

Apply Concepts

How would you prepare for severe weather in your area? Write a plan.

_____

_____

_____

_____

_____

_____

_____

_____

Take It Home!

Family Members: Work with your child to make a storm safety plan for your family.

SC.2.N.1.6 Explain how scientists . . . solve problems. SC.2.E.7.1 Compare and describe changing patterns in nature that repeat themselves . . . day to day and season to season. SC.2.E.7.5 State the importance of preparing for severe weather . . . .

Careers in Science

Ask a Storm Chaser

What kinds of storms do storm chasers look for?
Most storm chasers look for tornadoes. A few storm chasers look for hurricanes.

How do you work?
Storm chasers watch the weather carefully. We learn about bad storms. We try to predict where to find them. Then we drive to see a storm.

How does storm chasing help other people?
Most storm chasers work with weather centers. If we spot a storm, we can alert the police and people on farms.

Now It's Your Turn!

▶ What question would you ask a storm chaser?

_____

_____

Safety from the Storm

▶ Draw or write the answer to each question to get to safety.

1 Your family has a storm kit. You use it if you lose power or get hurt. Draw one thing you would put in a storm kit.

2 A storm might be coming. Why should you make a plan?

3 Storm chasers spot a tornado. Draw a picture of what they might see.

4 Tornado warning! Your family follows its safety plan by finding shelter. Why?

1

2
_____

_____

3

4
_____

_____

Name _____

Multiple Choice
Fill in the circle next to the best answer.

SC.2.E.7.2

1 Which does the sun warm the most in one hour?

Ⓐ air

Ⓑ soil

Ⓒ water

SC.2.E.7.4

2 Which picture shows wind?

Ⓐ

Ⓑ

Ⓒ

SC.2.P.8.1, SC.2.P.8.5

3 You measure the temperature at 10 in the morning during the week.

Monday	Tuesday	Wednesday
60 °F	68 °F	64 °F

Which is true?

Ⓐ Monday was hotter than Tuesday.

Ⓑ Tuesday was hotter than Monday.

Ⓒ Wednesday was hotter than Tuesday.

SC.2.E.7.1

④ Which is true of winter and spring?

Ⓐ Spring is usually colder than winter.

Ⓑ Winter is usually colder than spring.

Ⓒ Winter and spring usually have about the same temperatures.

SC.2.E.7.5

⑤ How do meteorologists help keep people safe from severe weather?

Ⓐ They name storms.

Ⓑ They stop severe weather.

Ⓒ They warn people about severe weather.

SC.2.N.1.1, SC.2.E.7.3

⑥ Oscar sets up this experiment with an open container of water.

What will he probably observe the next day?

Ⓐ There will be less water in the container.

Ⓑ There will be the same amount of water in the container.

Ⓒ There will be more water in the container.

UNIT 4
All About Matter

Big Idea 8

Properties of Matter

swimming in Florida

I Wonder Why

The floaties and the swim toys all keep their different shapes. Why?

Turn the page to find out.

Here's Why Gases take the shape of their container. This makes each object look different.

Big Idea 8 *Matter can have different properties. Matter can be a solid, a liquid, or a gas.*

Now I Get the Big Idea!

© Houghton Mifflin Harcourt Publishing Company (bkgd) ©Stockbyte/Getty Images; (t) ©Getty Images/Royalty Free; (border) ©NDisc/Age Fotostock

SC.2.P.8.1 Observe and measure objects in terms of their properties, including size, shape, color . . . weight, texture, sinking or floating in water . . . .

Essential Question

What Are Properties of Matter?

Engage Your Brain!

Look closely at the picture. Find the answer to the question in the lesson.

What is this a picture of?

It is _____.

Active Reading

Lesson Vocabulary

1 Preview the lesson.

2 Write the 5 vocabulary terms here.

_____ _____

_____ _____

_____

It All Matters

Objects around you are made of matter. **Matter** is anything that takes up space.

Matter has properties. A **property** is one part of what something is like. You can tell about objects by their properties. Some properties are size, shape, and color.

▶ Draw objects with different shapes on the bookshelves.

color   size   shape

Keep in Touch

Texture is another property of matter. **Texture** is the way something feels. The floor is hard. The cat's fur is soft. They have different textures. What other things feel hard or soft? What other words tell about texture?

▶ Draw something hard.   ▶ Draw something soft.

The floor is smooth, but the lamp shade is rough.

Measure Up!

You **measure** to find out about the size, weight, or amount of things.

Suppose you want to know the length of an object, or how long it is. You can measure length with a ruler, a meterstick, or a tape measure.

Do the Math!
Measure Length

Use a ruler to measure the lengths of objects. Write the names of three objects. Record the lengths in inches. Circle the name of the shortest object.

Length of Classroom Objects	
Object	Length in Inches

Worth the Weight

Why is it hard to lift a refrigerator? A refrigerator is heavy! An egg is easy to lift because it is light. **Weight** is a measure of how heavy something feels. A scale is used to measure the weight of an object.

▶ Draw a line from each fruit to the word that tells about its weight.

Light

Heavy

What Floats? What Sinks?

Look at the objects in the tub. The rubber duck floats. It stays on top of the water. The soap sinks. It falls to the bottom of the water. Which other objects in the tub float? Which other ones sink?

Active Reading

Opposites are words for things that are very different, such as light and heavy or stop and go. Draw triangles around two words on this page that are opposites.

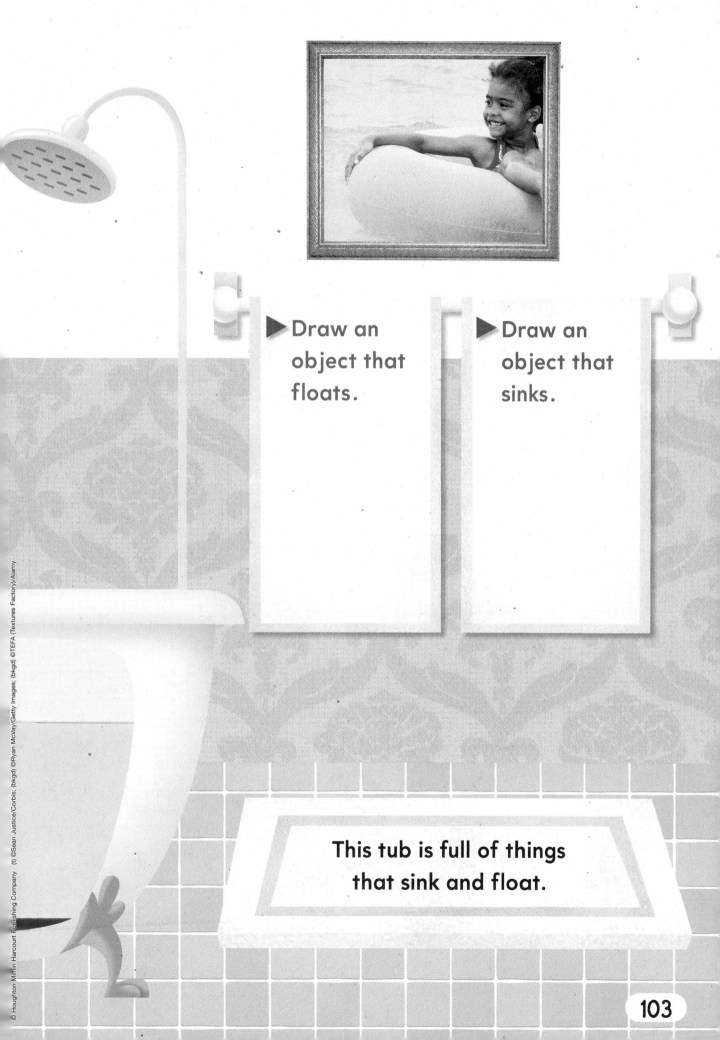

▶ Draw an object that floats.

▶ Draw an object that sinks.

This tub is full of things that sink and float.

Sum It Up!

1 Mark It!

Sort by properties. Draw an X on the object in each group that does not belong.

2 Circle It!

Circle the objects that sink.

Name _____

Word Play

Sort the words in the word bank. Write them in the chart. Show which words tell about each property of matter.

Properties of Matter

hard	heavy	round	small	soft
black	red	big	square	light

Size	Shape	Color	Texture	Weight

Apply Concepts

Tell about the properties of the beach ball. Write a word on each line to complete the word web.

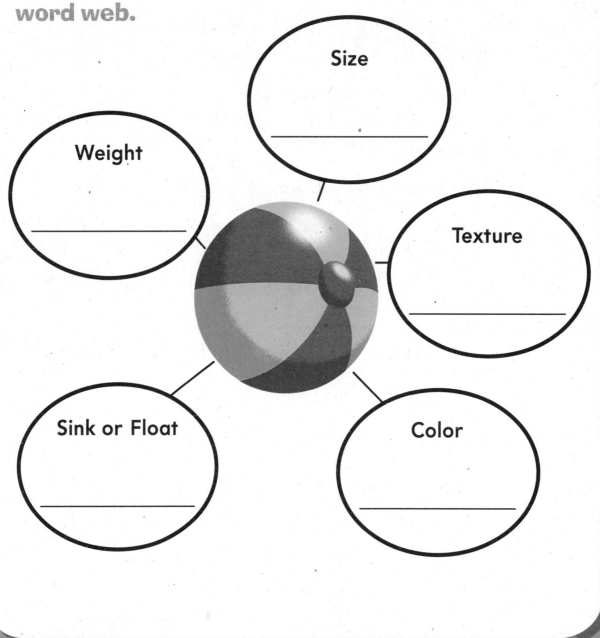

Size

_____

Weight

_____

Texture

_____

Sink or Float

_____

Color

_____

Family Members: Ask your child to tell you about properties of matter. Point out objects in your home. Have your child name two objects and their properties.

SC.2.N.1.1 Raise questions . . . investigate them in teams . . . and generate appropriate explanations based on those explorations. **SC.2.N.1.2** Compare the observations made by . . . using the same tools. **SC.2.N.1.3** Ask "how do you know?" in appropriate situations . . . . **SC.2.N.1.4** Explain how . . . scientific investigations should yield similar conclusions . . . . **SC.2.P.8.1** Observe and measure objects in terms of their properties, including size . . . weight . . . .

Name _____

Essential Question

How Can We Measure and Compare Objects?

Set a Purpose

Write what you will do in this investigation.

_____

_____

_____

Think About the Procedure

❶ How will you measure length? How will you measure weight?

_____

_____

❷ Why will you repeat the measurements?

_____

_____

Record Your Data

Record your results in the charts below. Remember to order the length from shortest to longest. Order the weight from lightest to heaviest.

Object	Length

Object	Weight

Draw Conclusions

Are longer objects always heavier?

_____

_____

Ask More Questions

What other questions can you ask about how to measure and compare objects?

_____

SC.2.P.8.2 Identify objects and materials as solid, liquid, or gas. SC.2.P.8.3 Recognize that solids have a definite shape and that liquids and gases take the shape of their container. SC.2.P.8.4 Observe and describe water in its solid, liquid, and gaseous states.

Lesson 3

Essential Question

What Are Solids, Liquids, and Gases?

Engage Your Brain!

Find the answer to the question in the lesson.

What is inside the balloon?

_____

Active Reading

Lesson Vocabulary

1 Preview the lesson.

2 Write the 5 vocabulary terms here.

_____   _____

_____   _____

_____

© Houghton Mifflin Harcourt Publishing Company   © Steve Allen/Brand X/Corbis

109

Matter Matters

You know that matter is anything that takes up space. Some things have more matter than others. **Mass** is the amount of matter in an object. This boy has more mass than his beach ball.

Solid, liquid, and gas are three states of matter. The boy's sunglasses are a solid. The water in his bottle is a liquid. The beach ball is filled with gases.

Active Reading

Find the sentence that tells the meaning of **mass**. Draw a line under the sentence.

What two states of matter make up the beach ball?

Solid as a Rock

Look at the chair, the towel, and the hat. How are these objects the same? The answer is that all three are solids.

A **solid** is the only state of matter that has its own shape. What other solids do you see in this picture?

▶ Draw a solid object that you would take to the beach.

Shape Up!

Is orange juice a solid? No. It does not have its own shape. If you pour juice from a pitcher in to a glass, its shape changes.

Juice is a liquid. A **liquid** is a state of matter that takes the shape of its container. What other liquids can you name?

▶ Color the empty glass to show the shape the liquid would take in it.

Salt water is a kind of liquid.

Life's a Gas

This girl is blowing air into the beach ball. Air is made up of gases. A **gas** is a state of matter that fills all the space in its container. The air will keep spreading out until it fills the entire beach ball.

You can't see air, but you can see and feel what it does.

Wonderful Water

On the outside of this glass, water vapor is becoming liquid water.

You can't see it, but water vapor is in the air around this glass.

There are three states of water—solid, liquid, and gas. The water we drink is a liquid. Solid water is ice. Water in the form of a gas is **water vapor**.

▶ What is water vapor?

_____

_____

States of Water

Write in each empty box to complete the chart.

Name	State	Shape
ice	solid	_____
water	_____	takes the shape of its container
_____	gas	fills up all the space in a container

1 Color It!

Color the solids red. Color the liquids blue. Color the gases yellow.

2 Write It!

Answer the question.

What do you call the three states of water?

_____

Word Play

Name _____

Write the word for each clue. Fill in the missing numbers in the table. Then decode the message.

a	b	c	d	e	f	g	h	i	j	k	l	m
11	26	4	16	8	25	9	13	23	6	14	20	19

n	o	p	q	r	s	t	u	v	w	x	y	z
7	18	1	3	22	21	17	2	15	10	5	12	24

takes the shape of its container

__ __ __ __ __ __
20 23 3 2 23 16

water in the form of a gas

__ __ __ __ __
15 11 1 18 22

amount of matter in an object

__ __ __ __
19 11 21 21

fills all the space of its container

__ __ __
9 11 21

__   __ __ __   __ __   __ __ __
11   16 11 12   11 17   17 13 8

__ __ __ __ __   __ __   __
26 8 11 4 13   23 21   11

__ __ __ __ __ __ __ __   __ __ __ __ __ __ !
20 11 2 9 13 23 7 9   19 11 17 17 8 22

Apply Concepts

Write or draw to fill in the chart with examples of solids, liquids, and gases.

Solids, Liquids, and Gases

Solids	Liquids	Gases
Ice	Water	(watherbason) Clouds
Jenny	chocolate milk	air
Shoe	Soda	Helium
Dress	honey	inside bubbles

Take It Home!

Family Members: As you and your child walk around your home, point out objects and materials. Have your child classify each one as a solid, a liquid, or a gas.

SC.2.N.1.6 Explain how scientists . . . are always investigating new ways to solve problems.
SC.2.P.8.2 Identify objects and materials as solid, liquid, or gas. SC.2.P.8.3 Recognize that
solids have a definite shape and that liquids and gases take the shape of their container.

People in Science

Get to Know...
Dr. Mario Molina

Dr. Mario Molina is a chemist, or a person who studies the properties of substances and how they interact. For many years he studied materials called chlorofluorocarbons (CFCs). CFCs were used in spray cans and refrigerators. Dr. Molina found that CFCs harm the ozone layer, a layer of gas around Earth. The ozone layer protects us from the sun's harmful rays.

Fun Fact

When Dr. Molina was a boy, he used a microscope to look at very tiny living things like this one.

119

This Leads to That

Dr. Molina and other scientists talked to lawmakers. They worked to get rid of CFCs in spray cans.

Now the ozone layer is coming back, thanks to Dr. Molina and others. In 1995, Dr. Molina won the Nobel Prize for his work.

▶ How did Dr. Molina's work help the environment?

_____

_____

Name _____

SC.2.N.1.1 Raise questions . . . investigate them in teams . . . and generate appropriate explanations based on those explorations. SC.2.N.1.2 Compare the observations made by different groups using the same tools. SC.2.P.8.6 Measure and compare the volume of liquids using containers of various shapes and sizes.

Essential Question

How Can We Compare Volumes?

Set a Purpose

Write what you will do in this investigation.

_____

State Your Hypothesis

Write your hypothesis, or the statement that you will test.

_____

_____

Think About the Procedure

How will you figure out which container is holding the most water?

_____

_____

_____

Record Your Data

In the chart, draw the shape of each container. Write in the amount that each container held.

Shape of Container	Amount of Water

Draw Conclusions

1 How did the shape of the container affect the way you thought about which one held more water?

_____

2 How did what you thought about each container compare with the actual results?

_____

_____

Ask More Questions

What other questions can you ask about volume?

_____

_____

Multiple Choice
Fill in the circle next to the best answer.

SC.2.N.1.2, SC.2.P.8.1

1 Mrs. Ruiz's class used this tool to weigh a rock.

The rock weighed four pounds. Ms. Turner's class used the tool to weigh the same rock.

What did Ms. Turner's class observe?

Ⓐ The rock weighed three pounds.

Ⓑ The rock weighed four pounds.

Ⓒ The rock weighed five pounds.

SC.2.N.1.3, SC.2.P.8.2

2 Taylor sees a balloon filled with air. She knows the air in the balloon is a gas. How does she know?

Ⓐ The air is warm.

Ⓑ The air fills all the space in the balloon.

Ⓒ The air has its own shape.

SC.2.P.8.2

3 Which object is a solid?

Ⓐ a penny

Ⓑ a puddle

Ⓒ a raindrop

SC.2.P.8.3

4 Which is true about all liquids?

Ⓐ All liquids take the shape of their container.

Ⓑ All liquids have their own shape.

Ⓒ All liquids are cold.

SC.2.P.8.4

5 Shane has some ice cubes in a glass. What state of matter are the ice cubes?

(A) gas

(B) liquid

(C) solid

SC.2.N.1.1, SC.2.N.1.2, SC.2.P.8.1

6 Kendra asks a question— How heavy is my cat?

Which tool should she use to answer her question?

(A) a ruler

(B) a scale

(C) a measuring cup

SC.2.N.1.4, SC.2.P.8.6

7 On Friday, Rashad measures how much water fills a water bottle. He observes that it holds 3 cups. On Sunday, he measures how much water fills the same bottle. How much water does the bottle hold on Sunday?

(A) 2 cups

(B) 3 cups

(C) 4 cups

Matter Can Change

© Houghton Mifflin Harcourt Publishing Company (bkgd) ©PhotoStock-Israel/Alamy; (inset) ©Ashley Jouhar/Getty Images; (border) ©NDisc/Age Fotostock

Big Idea 9

Changes in Matter

Florida oranges

I Wonder How

These oranges have been changed.
How?
Turn the page to find out.

125

Here's How Cutting an orange into pieces changes the orange's size and shape. Peeling an orange changes its size. Squeezing an orange causes its juice to come out.

Track Your Progress

Essential Questions and Florida Benchmarks

 Big Idea 9 *Matter can change in many ways. Not all matter can be changed in the same way.*

Now I Get the Big Idea!

SC.2.P.9.1 Investigate that materials can be altered to change some of their properties, but not all materials respond the same way to any one alteration.

Essential Question

How Does Matter Change?

Engage Your Brain!

Use words from the lesson to answer the question.

How does the artist make this sculpture?

She _____ water and then _____ the ice.

Active Reading

Lesson Vocabulary

1 Preview the lesson.

2 Write the 4 vocabulary terms here.

_____   _____

_____   _____

Deep Freeze

Think about making juice pops. You put juice in a freezer. The juice **freezes**, or turns from a liquid to a solid. You take the solid juice pops out of the freezer. They **melt**, or change to a liquid.

Not all things freeze or melt at the same temperature. Some liquids won't freeze in a freezer. A plastic bag won't melt if you leave it out of a freezer.

Active Reading

When you contrast, you tell ways in which things are different. Draw triangles around two words that are being contrasted.

This ice cream is frozen solid.

© Houghton Mifflin Harcourt Publishing Company

► Draw something that melts.

The ice cream melted, but the nuts and cherry did not melt.

Do the Math!
Compare Numbers

Circle the answers.

Ice cream melts faster when the air temperature is higher.

At which temperature will ice cream melt faster?

75 °F or **45 °F**

50 °F or **85 °F**

Time for a Change

When matter is cut or broken, its size and shape change. Matter also changes when it **dissolves**, or mixes completely with a liquid. Sugar, for example, dissolves in water. It spreads out and seems to disappear.

Changes to Matter

▶ Circle **yes** or **no** to answer the question in each row.

Can you dissolve it in water?
lemonade powder and sugar

yes   no

Can you cut it?
apple

yes   no

Can you break it?
egg

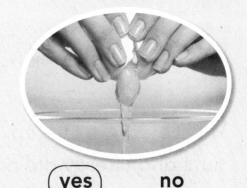

yes   no

salt

(yes)   no

spoon

yes   (no)

ruler

(yes)   (no)

paper

(yes)   no

crayon

(yes)   no

eraser

yes   (no)

Get Cooking

You know that heat cooks food. Cooking changes the food. The wood or coals in a grill burn to help cook the food. **Burning** means the changing of a substance into ashes and smoke. Cooking and burning are changes that make new kinds of matter.

Active Reading

Find the sentence that tells the meaning of **burning**. Draw a line under the sentence.

Cooking foods can change their color, size, shape, texture, smell, and taste.

▶ Write the change that is happening in each picture.

melting

Cooking.

Sum It Up!

① Circle It!

One picture shows a new kind of matter being made. Circle it.

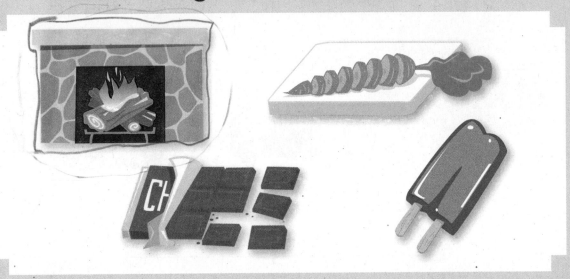

② Draw It!

Draw something before and after it melts.

Brain Check

Name _Sara_

Word Play

Read the label in each box. Write or draw two things you can change that way.

Freeze

icecin

Melt

Ice

Burn

Fire

Cut

her 3 paper

Answer the question.

What do burning and cooking do to matter?

_____

_____

Apply Concepts

In each box, write a word that tells the cause of the effect.

	Cause	Effect

juice pop → **melt** → juice

lemonade powder and sugar mixed in water → **diolve** → lemonade

water → **Freeze** → ice

© Houghton Mifflin Harcourt Publishing Company

SC.2.N.1.1 Raise questions . . . investigate them in teams . . . and generate appropriate explanations based on those explorations. **SC.2.N.1.3** Ask "how do you know?" in appropriate situations . . . . **SC.2.N.1.5** Distinguish between empirical observation . . . and ideas or inferences . . . . **SC.2.P.9.1** Investigate that materials can be altered . . . but not all materials respond the same way to any one alteration.

Name _____

Essential Question

How Can We Change Matter?

Set a Purpose

Write what you will do in this investigation.

_____

_____

Make a Prediction

Predict which substances will dissolve in the water.

_____

_____

Think About the Procedure

How do you know when a substance dissolves in water?

_____

_____

Record Your Data

Record your observations in this chart.

Substance	Prediction	Observation
salt		
sugar		
sand		
soil		

Draw Conclusions

Were your predictions correct?

_____

_____

Do all substances dissolve in water? Explain.

_____

_____

Ask More Questions

What other questions can you ask about dissolving?

_____

_____

© Houghton Mifflin Harcourt Publishing Company

SC.2.N.1.6 Explain how scientists alone or in groups are always investigating new ways to solve problems. SC.2.P.9.1 Investigate that materials can be altered to change some of their properties, but not all materials respond the same way to any one alteration.

People in Science

4 Things to Know About

Dr. Mei-Yin Chou

1 Dr. Chou was born in Taiwan. She studies physics. Physics is a science that tells about matter and energy.

2 She is a teacher at a university called Georgia Tech.

3 At Georgia Tech, Dr. Chou studies how gases affect solids.

4 She helps girls and women get involved in learning and teaching science.

Word Whiz

▶ **Write the words to match the clues.**

| Taiwan | physics | gases | women | Georgia Tech |

Across

3 Dr. Chou teaches at this university.

Down

1 Dr. Chou helps them learn about science.

2 This science tells about matter and energy.

4 Dr. Chou studies how these affect solids.

5 Dr. Chou was born in this country.

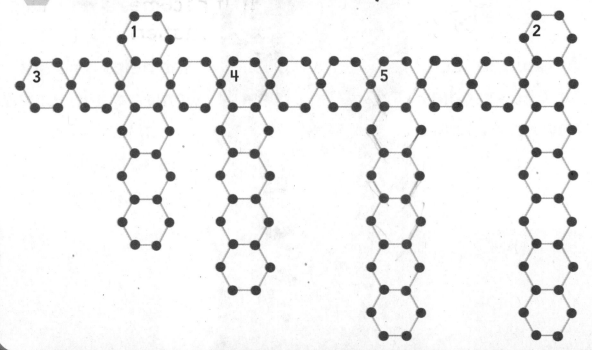

Name _Sara Mendez_

Multiple Choice
Fill in the circle next to the best answer.

SC.2.P.9.1

1 Which of these can you cut with scissors?

Ⓐ

Ⓑ

Ⓒ

SC.2.P.9.1

2 What happens when you mix and stir salt into water?

Ⓐ It dissolves.

Ⓑ It freezes.

Ⓒ It melts.

SC.2.P.9.1

3 How does matter change when it burns?

Ⓐ It turns from a solid to a liquid.

Ⓑ It mixes with a liquid.

Ⓒ It becomes a new kind of matter.

SC.2.N.1.3, SC.2.P.9.1

④ Ian stirs sand into a glass of warm water. He knows the sand is not dissolving in the water. How does he know?

Ⓐ All the sand sinks to the bottom of the glass.

Ⓑ The sand spreads out and mixes completely with the water.

Ⓒ The sand melts in the water.

SC.2.N.1.1, SC.2.N.1.5, SC.2.P.9.1

⑤ Things do not all act the same way when you freeze them. What will happen if you put a plastic bag in the freezer and then take it out?

Ⓐ The plastic bag would freeze but not melt.

Ⓑ The plastic bag would get cold but would not freeze or melt.

Ⓒ The plastic bag would freeze and melt.

UNIT 6
Energy

Big Idea 10

Forms of Energy

Miami skyline at night

I Wonder Why
The city looks very bright at night. Why?
Turn the page to find out.

Here's Why Electricity makes the city bright at night. It powers the lights in the buildings.

Track Your Progress

Essential Questions and Florida Benchmarks

Big Idea 10 *Energy is something that can cause matter to move or change. Energy has different forms.*

Now I Get the Big Idea!

SC.2.P.10.1 Discuss that people use electricity or other forms of energy to cook their food, cool or warm their homes, and power their cars.

Lesson 1

Essential Question

How Do We Use Energy?

Engage Your Brain!

Find the answer to the question in the lesson.

What makes the wheel move?

_____

makes it move.

Active Reading

Lesson Vocabulary

1 Preview the lesson.

2 Write the 5 vocabulary terms here.

water _____

_____ _____

_____

Full of Energy

It takes a lot of energy to power a city. **Energy** is something that can cause matter to move or change. Where do you see energy at work in this city?

Active Reading

Find the sentence that tells the meaning of **energy**. Draw a line under the sentence.

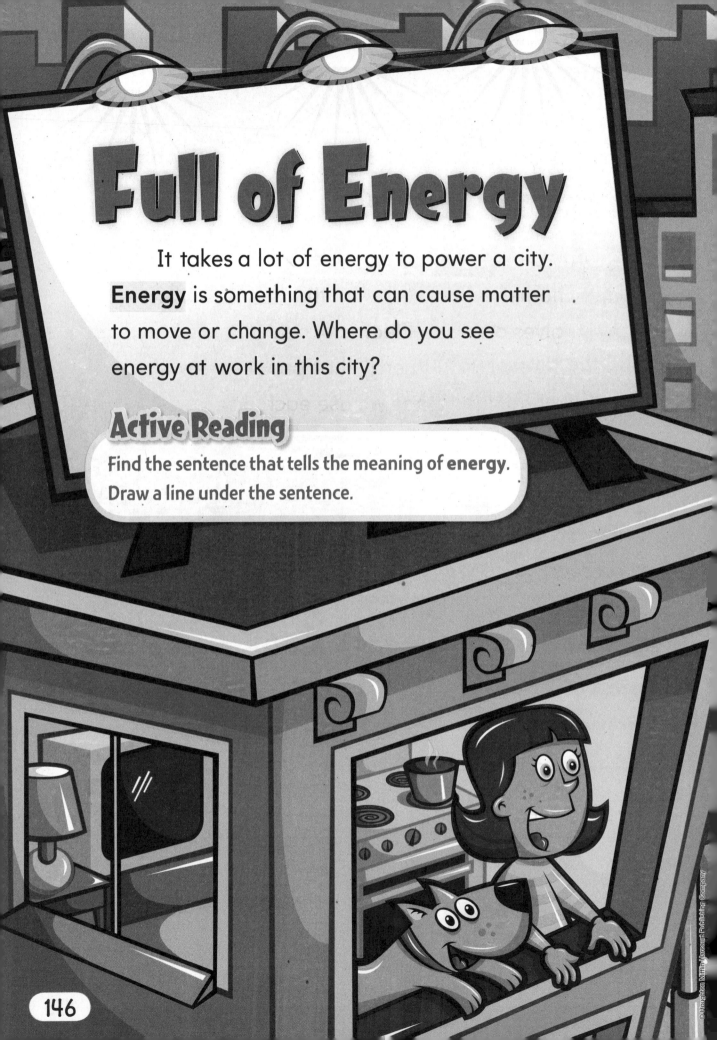

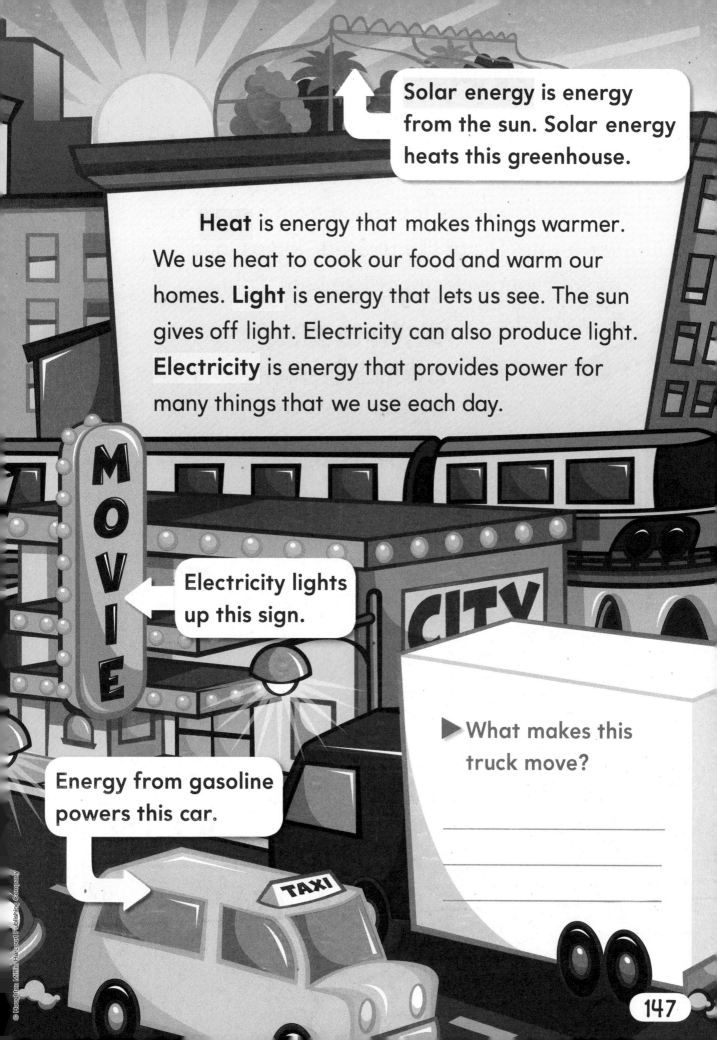

Solar energy is energy from the sun. Solar energy heats this greenhouse.

Heat is energy that makes things warmer. We use heat to cook our food and warm our homes. Light is energy that lets us see. The sun gives off light. Electricity can also produce light. Electricity is energy that provides power for many things that we use each day.

Electricity lights up this sign.

Energy from gasoline powers this car.

▶ What makes this truck move?

_____

_____

_____

Electricity at Home

Before school today, did you use a toaster to heat bread? Did you see by the light from a lamp? Did you use the sound from a radio to wake you? Things like toasters, lamps, and radios change electricity into heat, light, and sound.

Active Reading

As you read this page, circle the lesson vocabulary.

▶ Draw an X on something that lights the home.

Electricity moves from the outlet through the lamp.

© Houghton Mifflin Harcourt Publishing Company

The fan cools the people in the home.

The electric stove cooks food.

149

Kinds of Energy

Many kinds of energy provide power for the things we use each day. You can see some of these kinds of energy on these pages. People can use most of them to produce electricity.

This dam uses water to produce electricity.

▶ Name two kinds of energy that you see on these pages.

_____

_____

Wind turbines collect energy from wind.

Solar panels collect solar energy.

Do the Math!
Solve a Problem

Read the word problem. Answer the question.

There are 2 solar panels on each house. How many solar panels are there on 4 houses?

_____

Sum It Up!

1 Label It!

Look at the pictures. Complete the labels to tell why you use each thing.

to _cold_ people   to _het_ food   to _light_ a desk

2 Solve It!

Write the answer to the riddle.

I come from the sun
As light and heat.
I make things change—
It's really neat!

What am I?

3 Draw It!

Draw a way that you use electricity.

Brain Check

Name _____

Word Play

Write a word for each clue. Find each word in the word search. Then answer the question.

1. something that can make matter move or change _e n e r g y_

2. energy that lets us see _l i g h t_

3. energy from the sun _s o l a r_ energy

4. energy that makes things warmer _h e a t_

```
t  e  q  o  r  s  g  u  a
e  y  b  p  a  w  c  o  c
n  u  s  o  l  a  r  h  e
e  s  a  v  d  b  w  g  l
r  o  b  c  h  s  x  u  i
g  n  a  e  e  t  u  q  g
y  r  b  k  a  f  d  b  h
d  e  h  p  t  n  h  o  t
k  g  u  b  s  t  z  f  a
```

What kind of energy can be changed into light and heat? _____

153

Apply Concepts

Color yellow the things that light the house.
Color blue the things that cook food.
Circle all the things that use electricity.

Family Members: Ask your child to tell you about energy. Ask him or her to point out ways that energy is used around your home.

Take It Home!

SC.2.N.1.6 Explain how scientists alone or in groups are always investigating new ways to solve problems. SC.2.P.10.1 Discuss that people use electricity or other forms of energy to cook their food, cool or warm their homes, and power their cars.

4 Things to Know About Dr. Lawnie Taylor

1 Dr. Taylor studied physics. Physics is a science that tells about matter and energy.

2 He worked for the U.S. Department of Energy for many years.

3 He studied ways to use the sun's energy to heat homes and produce electricity.

4 Dr. Taylor also studied ways to use the sun's energy to make machines run.

157

Let the Sun Shine!

Dr. Taylor studied solar energy. Now you can, too!

▶ Write the number of each description next to the correct picture.

1 Solar panels on a house collect the sun's energy to produce electricity or heat water.

2 A solar farm can change the sun's energy into electricity for many people to use.

3 A solar car uses the sun's energy to make it run.

▶ How have you seen solar energy used?

_____

_____

Forces and Motion

Big Idea 8

Properties of Matter

Big Idea 13

Forces and Changes in Motion

water activities in Florida

I Wonder Why

The jet ski moves fast over the water. The canoe moves slowly. Why?

Turn the page to find out.

Here's Why Applying more force to an object will cause it to move faster.

Track Your Progress

Essential Questions and Florida Benchmarks

Big Idea 8 *Magnets attract some objects and repel others.*

Big Idea 13 *Forces can make objects move. Magnets can move some objects without touching them.*

Now I Get the Big Idea!

SC.2.P.13.1 Investigate the effect of . . . pushes and pulls . . . . SC.2.P.13.3 Recognize that objects are pulled toward the ground unless something holds them up.
SC.2.P.13.4 Demonstrate that the greater the force . . . applied to an object, the greater the change in motion of the object.

Essential Question

What Are Forces?

Engage Your Brain!

Find the answer to the question in the lesson.

The chair is holding up the circus star. What force is pulling down on him?

_____ is pulling down on him.

Active Reading

Lesson Vocabulary

1 Preview the lesson.

2 Write the 5 vocabulary terms here.

_____   _____

_____   _____

_____

In Full Force

This rope is moving round and round. It is in motion. **Motion** means movement. Something that is moving is in motion.

A juggler makes rings move in different ways. The juggler uses forces to change their motion. A **force** is a push or a pull. How do you use forces to change motion?

Active Reading

Find the sentence that tells the meaning of **force**. Draw a line under the sentence.

A **push** is a force that moves something away from you. A **pull** is a force that moves something toward you.

The juggler uses pushes and pulls to change how the rings move.

▶ Draw a push or a pull.

Up to Speed

How do acrobats fly through the air? They use forces to change their speed and direction. **Speed** is how fast something moves. A small force changes an object's speed and direction a little. A large force can change them a lot.

The acrobats are using forces to change direction.

▶ What happens to the speed of the cart if you give it a big push?

_____

_____

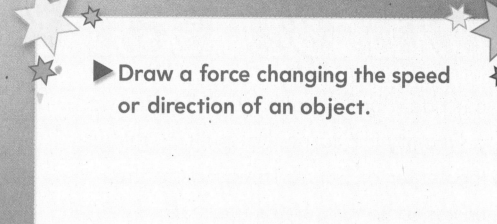

▶ Draw a force changing the speed or direction of an object.

The harder the acrobats push and pull, the faster they go.

Down to Earth

If you drop a ball, it falls. Why? The answer is gravity. **Gravity** is a force that pulls all things toward the center of Earth. Things fall to the ground unless something holds them up.

Active Reading

A detail is a fact about a main idea. Draw one line under a detail about gravity. Draw an arrow to the main idea it tells about.

▶ Put an X on the object holding this man up.

When the unicycle moves, there is friction between the wheel and the ground.

▶ Rub your hands together fast and hard. Tell how you know that there is friction.

_____

Slow Down!

Think about riding your bike. You might not know it, but friction is at work between the tires and the road. **Friction** is a force that slows or stops things that are touching. Friction also causes objects to get warmer when they rub together. How does friction affect the bike?

Sum It Up!

1 Label It!

Write push or pull to label each picture.

Push

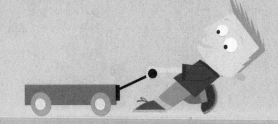

Pull

2 Solve It!

Write the answer to the riddle.

You can't see me, but I am a force. I pull things to Earth— a pen, an egg, or even a horse!

What am I?

gravaty

3 Circle It!

Circle the answer.

Jay pushes a box with a little force. Then he pushes it with a lot more force. How will he change the box's speed?

The box goes _____ faster.

much   a little

SC.2.N.1.1 Raise questions . . . investigate them in teams . . . and generate appropriate explanations based on those explorations. SC.2.N.1.3 Ask "how do you know?" in appropriate situations . . . . SC.2.N.1.5 Distinguish between empirical observation . . . and ideas or inferences . . . . SC.2.P.13.1 Investigate the effect of . . . pushes and pulls . . . . SC.2.P.13.4 Demonstrate that the greater the force . . . applied to an object, the greater the change in motion of the object.

Name _____

Essential Question

How Do Forces Make Objects Move?

Set a Purpose

Write what you want to find out.

_____

_____

State Your Hypothesis

Write your hypothesis, or the statement that you will test.

_____

_____

Think About the Procedure

How does measuring time tell you about speed?

_____

_____

Record Your Data

Record your observations in this chart.

Force	Amount of Time
less force	
more force	

Draw Conclusions

1 How does the amount of time change when the force is greater?

_____

_____

2 How does the speed change when the force is greater? How do you know?

_____

_____

Ask More Questions

What other questions can you ask about how force changes the motion of objects?

_____

_____

Ask a Roller Coaster Designer

What do roller coaster designers do?
We design roller coasters for amusement parks. We think up ideas for new rides. We also figure out how much they will cost to build.

Do designers work alone?
We work as a team with engineers to make a design. The design has to work and be safe and fun for riders. A factory then builds the ride.

How long does it take to build a roller coaster?
It usually takes about a year from design to finish. A simpler design takes less time.

Now It's Your Turn!

▶ What question would you ask a roller coaster designer?

_____

_____

_____

_____

Design Your Own Roller Coaster

▶ Draw your own roller coaster in the space below.

▶ Explain your design. Write about how your roller coaster moves.

_____

_____

_____

Name _____

SC.2.N.1.1 Raise questions . . . investigate them in teams . . . . SC.2.N.1.2 Compare the observations made by different groups using the same tools. SC.2.N.1.3 Ask "how do you know?" in appropriate situations . . . . SC.2.P.8.1 Observe and measure objects in terms of their properties, including . . . attraction and repulsion of magnets. SC.2.P.13.2 Demonstrate that magnets can be used to make some things move without touching them.

Essential Question

How Strong Is a Magnet?

Set a Purpose

Write what you want to find out.

_____

_____

State Your Hypothesis

Write your hypothesis, or the statement that you will test.

_____

_____

Think About the Procedure

Why is it important to test the strength of the magnet with different classroom objects?

_____

_____

Record Your Data

Record your observations in this chart. Write the names of the three objects you tested. Circle **attracts** or **does not attract** based on your results.

Object	Attracts/Does Not Attract	
piece of paper	attracts	does not attract
object 2	attracts	does not attract
object 3	attracts	does not attract
object 4	attracts	does not attract

Draw Conclusions

1 How does putting something between the magnet and the paper clip affect the strength of the magnet?

_____

_____

2 Why do you think that happens?

_____

Ask More Questions

What other questions can you ask about magnets?

_____

Multiple Choice

Fill in the circle next to the best answer.

SC.2.N.1.1, SC.2.P.13.1,
SC.2.P.13.4

1 What happens if you use a small force to push a large, heavy wagon?

(A) It moves very fast.

(B) It moves a lot.

(C) It moves a little.

SC.2.P.8.1, SC.2.P.13.2

2 What holds the paper clip up?

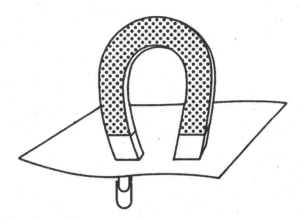

(A) gravity

(B) a magnetic field

(C) the paper

SC.2.P.13.3

3 Which force makes the ball roll down the hill?

(A) friction

(B) gravity

(C) motion

SC.2.N.1.2, SC.2.P.8.1

4 Two groups of students do an experiment to see whether a magnet attracts steel paper clips. The groups use the same type of magnet and the same type of steel paper clips. What will their results be?

(A) Both groups will find that the magnet attracts the paper clips.

(B) Both groups will find that the magnet does not attract the paper clips.

(C) The groups will have different results.

SC.2.N.1.1, SC.2.N.1.5, SC.2.P.13.4

5 You blow softly on a ball. The ball crosses a finish line in 8 seconds. You blow hard on the ball. The ball crosses the finish line in 3 seconds. Which of the following can you infer from the activity?

(A) The amount of force affects motion.

(B) The amount of force does not affect motion.

(C) You cannot use force to move an object.

UNIT 8
The Human Body

Big Idea 14

Organization and Development of Living Organisms

surfing in Florida

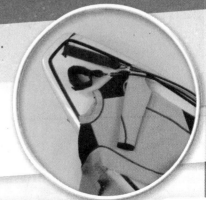

I Wonder Why

It is important to wear safety gear when exercising. Why?

Turn the page to find out.

Here's Why Safety gear protects your muscles, bones, and other body parts.

Track Your Progress

Essential Questions and Florida Benchmarks

Big Idea 14 *Humans have body parts that keep them alive. Each body part has a particular job to do.*

Now I Get the Big Idea!

Lesson 1

Essential Question

What Makes Up the Human Body?

Engage Your Brain!

Find the answer to the riddle in the lesson.

Your hand has about 27 of these. They help your hand move.

They are _____ .

Active Reading

Lesson Vocabulary

1 Preview the lesson.

2 Write the 6 vocabulary terms here.

_____   _____

_____   _____

_____   _____

Your Body

Starring Your Brain

brain

Your body is amazing! It has many parts. The parts work together. They help keep you alive.

Your **brain** is one important body part. Your brain tells your other body parts what to do. Your brain lets you think, remember, and feel.

Active Reading

Find the sentences that tell what your brain does. Draw a line under the sentences.

Your Stomach

When you swallow, food moves from your mouth through a tube called the esophagus. Then the food moves into your stomach.

Your **stomach** helps digest, or break down, food. Your body uses the nutrients in the food. Then you can run, play, and think.

stomach

▶ Name a food that helps your body.

Your Skeleton and Muscles

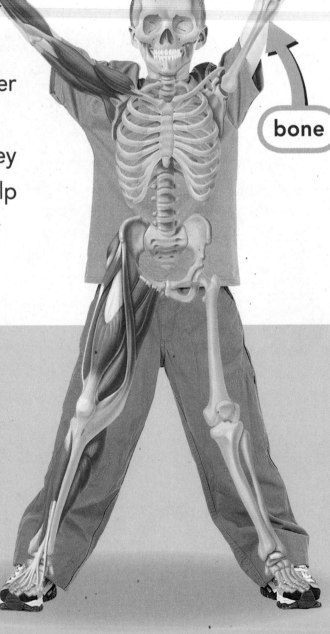

muscle

bone

Your body has many bones. All your bones together form your **skeleton**. Some bones hold up your body. They give your body shape and help it move. Other bones protect parts inside your body.

Active Reading

A detail is a fact about a main idea. Draw a line under a detail about bones.

You have **muscles** all over your body. Some muscles pull on your bones to move them. Other muscles move things like nutrients and oxygen through your body.

Muscles and bones work together.

▶ How do your bones and muscles work together?

_____

_____

Your Lungs

Your lungs are in your chest.

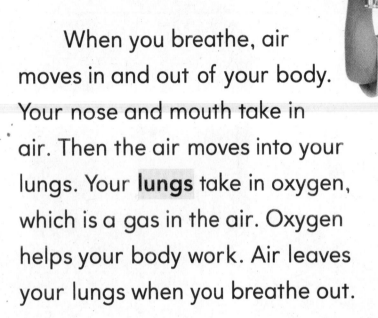

When you breathe, air moves in and out of your body. Your nose and mouth take in air. Then the air moves into your lungs. Your **lungs** take in oxygen, which is a gas in the air. Oxygen helps your body work. Air leaves your lungs when you breathe out.

► Draw your lungs. Then draw arrows to show how air moves into your lungs.

Your Heart

Your **heart** is a muscle. It pushes blood through your body. Blood carries oxygen and other things to all parts of your body. Your heart works all the time to keep your blood flowing.

Your heart is in your chest, too.

▶ Why is it important for your heart to beat all the time?

_____

_____

A Healthy Heart

Exercise is good for your body. Do you know why? One reason is that exercise keeps your heart strong.

Every time your heart beats, it pumps blood through your body. Exercise makes your heart beat faster and work harder. Over time, all this work makes your heart strong.

Do the Math!

Take a Survey

Ask classmates which of these kinds of exercise they like the best. Use tallies to show their votes. Group your marks in fives.

Example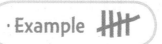

Exercises We Like	Total
Running	
Basketball	
Swimming	
Soccer	

Skip-count to find the total for each exercise. Then answer the questions.

1. Which exercise did most students like?

_____

2. How many votes did it get?

_____

Sum It Up!

① Circle It!

Circle the words that tell about lungs.

breathe

think

food

air

② Write It!

Complete the poem.

I'm in charge of all your parts.
I'm the reason you are smart.
When you're at school, at play, or in bed,
I'm your _____, and I'm in your head!

③ Draw It!

Draw yourself doing an exercise that helps keep your heart strong.

Name _____

Word Play

Label the body parts. Use each word in the word bank.

| brain | heart | lungs | stomach | bone | muscle |

Apply Concepts

Fill in the chart. Show what you know about the parts of your body.

My Body

Part	What It Does
stomach	_____
_____	work with my bones to help me move
skeleton	_____
_____	help me breathe

Take It Home!

Family Members: Ask your child to tell you what his or her stomach does. Then talk about favorite foods. Have your child name favorite foods that are also healthful.

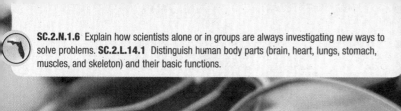

People in Science

Get to Know...
Dr. Patricia Bath

Dr. Patricia Bath is an eye doctor. She invented a machine that helps her operate on eyes. It uses a laser to remove cataracts. Cataracts can make a person's vision cloudy. They can even make people blind. Dr. Bath's machine has helped many people see again.

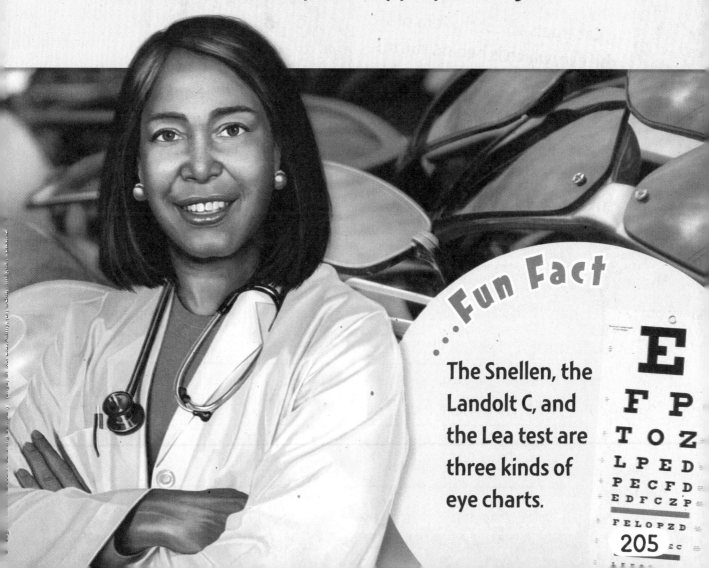

...Fun Fact

The Snellen, the Landolt C, and the Lea test are three kinds of eye charts.

E
F P
T O Z
L P E D
P E C F D
E D F C Z P
F E L O P Z D

205

This Leads to That

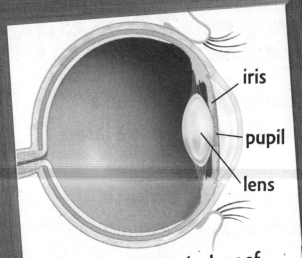

iris

pupil

lens

Cataracts affect the lens of the eye, which is behind the iris and the pupil. Dr. Bath's machine removes cataracts to help improve vision.

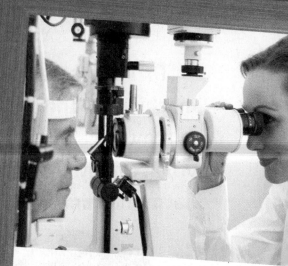

Dr. Bath still works to help people get better eye care. Here an eye doctor gives an older patient a checkup.

▶ What question would you ask Dr. Bath about her work?

_____

_____

_____

Name _____

SC.2.N.1.1 Raise questions . . . investigate them in teams . . . and generate appropriate explanations based on those explorations. **SC.2.N.1.3** Ask "how do you know?" in appropriate situations . . . . **SC.2.N.1.4** Explain how . . . scientific investigations should yield similar conclusions . . . . **SC.2.L.14.1** Distinguish human body parts (brain, heart, lungs, stomach, muscles, and skeleton) and their basic functions.

Essential Question

What Changes Your Heart Rate?

Set a Purpose

Write what you want to find out.

_____

_____

State Your Hypothesis

Write your hypothesis, or the statement that you will test.

_____

_____

Think About the Procedure

How will you test the change in your heart rate?

_____

_____

207

Record Your Data

In this chart, record what you observe.

	Before Exercise	After Exercise
number of heartbeats in 15 seconds	_____	_____

Draw Conclusions

How does exercise change your heart rate? How do you know?

_____

_____

_____

Ask More Questions

How else could you test changes in your heart rate?

_____

_____

_____

Name _____

Multiple Choice

Fill in the circle next to the best answer.

SC.2.L.14.1

1 Look at the picture.

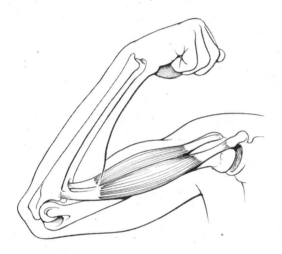

What do these body parts do?

Ⓐ They help you breathe.

Ⓑ They help you move.

Ⓒ They help you digest food.

SC.2.L.14.1

2 Look at the picture.

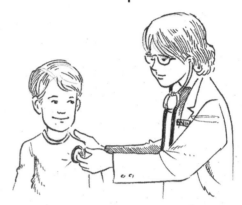

Which body part is this doctor checking?

Ⓐ the brain

Ⓑ the lungs

Ⓒ the skeleton

SC.2.L.14.1

3 How do the esophagus and stomach work?

Ⓐ Food moves from the stomach to the esophagus.

Ⓑ Air moves from the esophagus to the stomach.

Ⓒ Food moves from the esophagus to the stomach.

SC.2.L.14.1

❹ Which body part helps you think, remember, and feel?

Ⓐ the brain

Ⓑ the heart

Ⓒ the lungs

SC.2.N.1.1, SC.2.N.1.3, SC.2.L.14.1

❺ Your heart rate changes when you exercise. How do you know?

Ⓐ You predict that your heart rate changes when you exercise.

Ⓑ You feel tired after you exercise.

Ⓒ You measure your heart rate before and after you exercise.

SC.2.N.1.1, SC.2.N.1.4, SC.2.L.14.1

❻ A doctor checks Miguel's heart rate while he is at rest. Then she checks it a second time while he is still at rest. She does not change the way she does the test. What should the results of the second test be?

Ⓐ Miguel's heart rate should be about the same.

Ⓑ Miguel's heart rate should be much faster.

Ⓒ Miguel's heart rate should be much slower.

UNIT 9
Life Cycles

Big Idea 16

Heredity and Reproduction

sea turtles

I Wonder Why

Mother sea turtles bury their eggs in the sand. Why?

Turn the page to find out.

Here's Why Mother turtles need to keep their eggs warm and protected for the young turtles to hatch.

Track Your Progress

Essential Questions and Florida Benchmarks

Big Idea 16 *All organisms have a life cycle. Many young plants and animals look like their parents, but some do not.*

Now I Get the Big Idea!

© Houghton Mifflin Harcourt Publishing Company (bkgd) ©Marco Simoni/Getty Images; (t) ©Richard Bluschart/Alamy; (c) ©Neal Hicks/Alamy; (border) ©NDisc/Age Fotostock

SC.2.L.16.1 Observe and describe major stages in the life cycles of plants and animals, including beans and butterflies.

Essential Question

What Are Some Animal Life Cycles?

Engage Your Brain!

Find the answer to the riddle in this lesson.

When is a frog not like a frog?

When it is

a _____.

 **Active Reading**

Lesson Vocabulary

1 Preview the lesson.

2 Write the 6 vocabulary terms here.

_____   _____

_____   _____

_____   _____

Animal Start-Ups

A dog can have puppies. A cat can have kittens. Adult animals can **reproduce**, or have young. Animals such as puppies and kittens look like their parents. How does a kitten look like an adult cat?

Other young animals look very different from their parents. They go through changes and become like their parents.

A young cat looks like its parents.

A young butterfly does not look like its parents.

▶ Name another animal that looks like its parents.

_____

What's in the Egg?

Many animals begin life by hatching from an egg. Animals change as they grow. The changes that happen to an animal during its life make up its **life cycle**.

▶ How are the animals in this chart alike?

_____

_____

Animal Life Cycles

Kind of Animal	Egg	Young	Adult
Chicken			
Turtle			
Rainbow Trout			

Egg

A frog begins life inside a tiny egg.

Young Tadpole

A tadpole hatches from the egg. It lives in water. It takes in oxygen with gills.

Hatch, Swim, Hop

Did you know that a frog begins life inside a tiny egg? The young frog goes through changes to become an adult. These changes are called **metamorphosis**.

Active Reading

Circle the name of the body parts that a tadpole uses to take in oxygen. Underline the name of the body parts that an adult frog uses to take in oxygen.

Growing Tadpole

The tadpole gets bigger. It grows four legs. Later, it loses its tail.

Frog

The adult can live on land or in the water. It hops. It breathes with lungs.

217

Polar Parenting

It is late October. A female polar bear gets a shelter ready for her cubs. She digs a den in the snow. The den will keep her young warm and safe. She gives birth in winter.

▶ How is a polar bear's life cycle different from a frog's life cycle?

_____

1

2

Newborn

A polar bear cub is born inside the den. It drinks milk from its mother's body.

Growing Cub

The cub begins to explore outside the den.

We'll stay with our mother for almost three years, until we're grown up.

3

4

Young Polar Bear

The young polar bear learns to swim and hunt.

Adult Polar Bear

The adult polar bear can live on its own. It can have its own young.

The Mighty Monarch

A monarch butterfly has a life cycle, too. An adult female butterfly lays a tiny egg. The egg is so small it is hard to see. This picture shows a close-up of an egg on a leaf.

1 egg

► Why do you think a butterfly egg is so small?

_____

_____

2 larva

A tiny **larva**, or caterpillar, hatches from the egg. A caterpillar is a young butterfly. The larva eats a lot and grows quickly.

Then the larva stops eating and moving. The larva becomes a pupa. It makes a hard covering.

A **pupa** goes through metamorphosis inside the covering. It grows wings. Many other changes also happen.

3 pupa

4 adult

Finally, an adult butterfly comes out of the covering. It can have its own young.

Active Reading

Clue words can help you find the order of events. Draw a box around the clue words **then** and **finally**.

Sum It Up!

① Mark It!

Draw an X on the animal that does not look like its young.

② Draw It!

Draw a picture of this animal's mother.

③ Solve It!

Answer the riddle.

I am little now.

I will change and grow.

Someday I will be an adult cat.

What am I? _____

④ Think About It!

Is a  most like a

 , a , or

a  ? Why?

Name _____

Word Play

Use these words to complete the puzzle.

| tadpole | change | pupa | larva | reproduce | cycle |

Across

1. The stage in a butterfly's life cycle after the egg

2. To make more living things of the same kind

Down

3. The stage in a butterfly's life between larva and adult

4. A young frog that lives in water

5. This takes place during metamorphosis in frogs and butterflies

6. All the stages of an animal's life make up its life _____.

Apply Concepts

How is the life cycle of a butterfly different from the life cycle of a polar bear? Use this chart to show your answer.

Life Cycles

Butterfly	Polar Bear
A butterfly hatches from an egg.	_____ _____
_____ _____	A polar bear cub drinks milk from its mother's body.
_____ _____	A polar bear cub looks a lot like its parents.
A butterfly larva does not stay with its parents.	_____ _____

Take It Home!

Family Members: Discuss life cycles with your child. Sort family photographs to show ways that your child and others have grown and changed over the years.

Learn About ...
Salim Ali

Salim Ali is called the "Birdman of India." He traveled around India to study birds in their habitats. Ali discovered some kinds of birds. He wrote books about the birds he observed. Many people enjoyed reading his books.

...Fun Fact

Bird watchers use binoculars like these to see birds more closely.

Watch the Bird Grow!

Salim Ali learned about birds. You can learn about birds, too.

▶ Order the life cycle of a robin. Number the pictures from 1 to 4.

young robin

adult robin

robin chick

robin eggs

▶ How is a robin's life cycle like the life cycles of other animals you know?

_____

_____

_____

_____

_____

_____

SC.2.N.1.1 Raise questions . . . investigate them in teams . . . and generate appropriate explanations based on those explorations. **SC.2.N.1.3** Ask "how do you know?" in appropriate situations . . . . **SC.2.L.16.1** Observe and describe major stages in the life cycles of plants and animals, including beans and butterflies.

Name _____

Essential Question

How Does a Bean Plant Grow?

Set a Purpose

Explain what you will learn from this activity.

_____

_____

Think About the Procedure

1 Why must you give the plant water and sunlight?

_____

_____

2 Compare the way that your bean plant grew with the way that a classmate's bean plant grew. What was the same?

_____

_____

Record Your Data

In this chart, record what you observe.

Date	Observations

Draw Conclusions

How did the bean plant change?

_____

_____

_____

Ask More Questions

What other questions could you ask about how plants grow?

_____

_____

228

SC.2.L.16.1 Observe and describe major stages in the life cycles of plants and animals, including beans and butterflies.

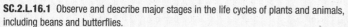

Lesson **3**

Essential Question

What Are Some Plant Life Cycles?

Engage Your Brain!

Find the answer to the question in this lesson.

What does the flower part of a dandelion make?

It makes

_____ .

Active Reading

Lesson Vocabulary

① Preview the lesson.

② Write the 4 vocabulary terms here.

_____   _____

_____   _____

Plant Start-Ups

Plants are living things. They grow and change. They have life cycles. Most plant life cycles begin with a **seed**. New plants grow from seeds. The growing plants start to look like their parent plants.

Active Reading

Find the words that tell about seeds. Draw a line under the words.

The plants in this garden grew from seeds.

How Fast Do Plants Grow?

Some plants grow quickly. Plants in a vegetable garden take just a few months to become adult plants. Other plants, such as trees, take many years to become adults.

Do the Math!

Interpret a Table

Use the chart to answer the question.

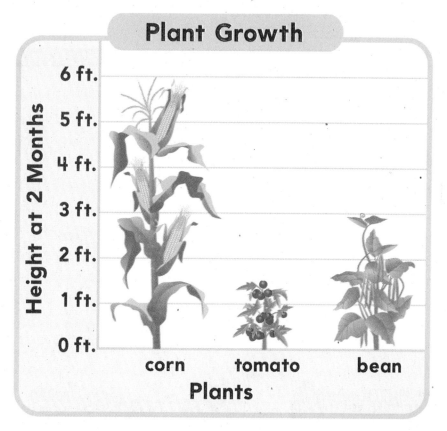

Plant Growth

▶ How much taller did the corn plant grow than the bean plant?

Start with a Seed

What happens when you plant a seed? When a seed gets warmth, air, and water, it may germinate. **Germinate** means to start to grow. The stem of the tiny plant breaks through the ground. The plant gets taller and grows leaves.

▶ Which plant parts grow from the seed first?

_____

A tiny plant is inside a seed.

The seed germinates. The roots grow down.

The stem grows up toward the light.

Growing Up

The tiny plant inside the seed has become a young plant called a **seedling**.

The seedling grows into an adult plant. An adult plant can make flowers and seeds.

Active Reading

Find the words that tell the meaning of **seedling**. Draw a line under those words.

The plant grows more roots and leaves.

The adult plant grows flowers.

Apples
All Around

Some plants have flowers that make seeds and fruit. Parts of the flower grow into fruit. The fruit grows around the seeds to hold and protect them.

Active Reading

Circle the word **seeds** each time you see it on these two pages.

apple blossoms

Parts of apple blossoms grow into apples. The apples grow around seeds.

A Long Life

Some plants have short lives. They die soon after their flowers make seeds. Other plants, such as apple trees, can live for many years. An apple tree can live for a hundred years or more!

adult apple tree

► What do apple blossoms make?

Inside a Cone

Some plants, like pine trees, do not have flowers. But they do have seeds. Where do their seeds grow? A **cone** is a part of a pine tree and some other plants. Seeds grow inside the cone.

closed pinecones

open pinecones with seeds

The cone protects the seeds until they are ready to germinate. Then the cone opens up, and the seeds can fall out.

▶ Where do pine seeds form?

Pine Tree Beginnings

Pine seeds fall to the ground and germinate. As the seedlings grow, they start to look like their parent plants. After a few years, the pine trees grow cones and make seeds. The life cycle begins again.

adult pine trees

▶ What happens after an adult pine tree grows cones and makes seeds?

_____

_____

Sum It Up!

1 Draw It!

Draw the missing step in the plant's life cycle. Label your picture.

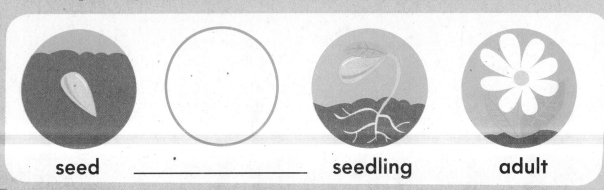

seed _____ seedling   adult

2 Mark It!

Draw an X on the plant part that does not have seeds.

3 Think About It!

How are flowers and pinecones alike?

_____

_____

 # Brain Check

Lesson **3**

Name _____

Word Play

Read each word. Trace a path through the maze to connect each word to its picture.

| seed | cone | flower | seedling |

Apply Concepts

Write to tell about the life cycle of a plant. Use the words <u>germinate</u>, <u>seed</u>, and <u>seedling</u>.

Life Cycle of a Plant

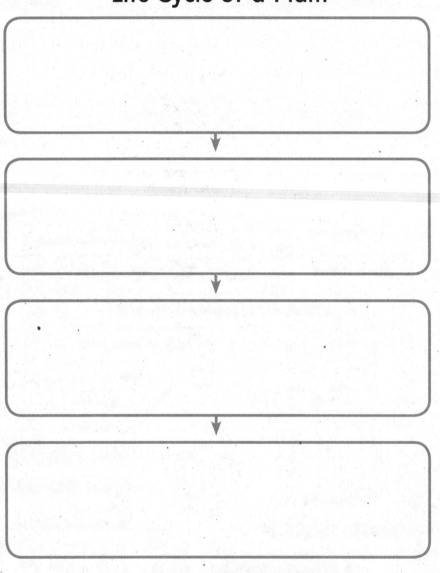

Family Members: Ask your child to tell you about plant life cycles. Then take a walk around your neighborhood. Talk about the plants you see.

© Houghton Mifflin Harcourt Publishing Company

Name _____

Multiple Choice

Fill in the circle next to the best answer.

SC.2.L.16.1

1 Which animal hatches from an egg?

Ⓐ

Ⓑ

Ⓒ

SC.2.L.16.1

2 During which stage of a butterfly's life cycle does the butterfly make a hard covering?

Ⓐ egg

Ⓑ larva

Ⓒ pupa

SC.2.L.16.1

3 How are the life cycles of an apple tree and a pine tree the same?

Ⓐ They both have flowers that grow into fruits.

Ⓑ They both have cones that hold seeds.

Ⓒ They both make seeds.

SC.2.L.16.1

4 Which shows the correct order of the life cycle of a bean plant?

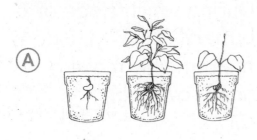

(A)

(B)

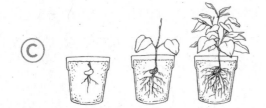

(C)

SC.2.N.1.1, SC.2.N.1.3, SC.2.L.16.1

5 Gabriel is looking at this plant in his backyard.

He knows it is an adult plant. How does he know?

(A) The plant has leaves.

(B) The plant has a flower.

(C) The plant has a stem.

SC.2.L.16.1

6 What helps a tadpole take in oxygen?

(A) gills

(B) lungs

(C) tail

UNIT 10
Basic Needs and Environments

Big Idea 17

Interdependence

manatees in Crystal River

I Wonder Why
**This manatee is eating underwater.
Why?** *Turn the page to find out.*

Here's Why Manatees live in water environments. They eat plants that grow underwater.

Big Idea 17 *Plants and animals, including humans, have basic needs. Living things can survive only in environments where their needs can be met.*

Now I Get the Big Idea!

SC.2.L.17.1 Compare and contrast the basic needs that all living things, including humans, have for survival.

Lesson 1

Essential Question

What Are Plant Needs?

🧠 Engage Your Brain!

Find the answer to the question in the lesson.

What do you know about a pumpkin this big?

Its _____ were met.

Active Reading

Lesson Vocabulary

1 Preview the lesson.

2 Write the 2 vocabulary terms here.

_____ _____

Plant Needs

Plants are living things. All living things must have certain things to live and grow. These things are called **basic needs**. What happens if a plant does not meet its basic needs? It may stop growing. It may turn brown or begin to droop. It may die.

Active Reading

Circle details that tell what happens when a plant does not meet its basic needs.

These plants are meeting their basic needs.

▶ What basic need is the boy giving the plants?

_____

People can help plants meet their basic needs.

Wonderful Water

Plants need water. Do you know how they get it? A plant's roots take in water from the soil. Water is a basic need that helps plants live and grow.

Light and Airy

Do you wonder why people put some potted plants by windows? Plants need sunlight to grow. They also need air and water. Plants use air, water, and sunlight to make their own food.

Active Reading

Underline the sentence that tells what plants need to make food.

How are these plants getting what they need?

Nutrients and Space

Plants need nutrients from the soil. **Nutrients** are substances that help plants grow. Growing plants need more nutrients and water. Their roots grow and spread to get more of these things. Plants need enough space for their roots, stems, and leaves to grow.

▶ Circle the place that shows that these tomato plants have space to grow.

Sum It Up!

1 Mark It!

Cross out the thing that a plant does **not** need to grow.

2 Solve It!

Fill in the blank.

I am all around you but you can't see me. I am something all living things need.
What am I?

_____

3 Draw It!

Draw a picture of a plant. Label the picture to show that the plant is getting what it needs.

Brain Check

Lesson **1**

Name _____

Word Play

Find and circle the words in this word search. Then answer the question.

sunlight	water	soil	air	space	nutrients

```
s  u  n  l  i  g  h  t  a  s
p  a  e  k  w  a  t  r  b  o
a  i  r  y  a  n  s  o  i  l
c  p  c  e  t  l  d  o  u  i
e  t  s  p  e  c  a  t  m  n
a  n  u  t  r  i  e  n  t  s
```

What are the things that plants must meet to live and grow?

_____

251

Complete the word web to tell about the things that plants need.

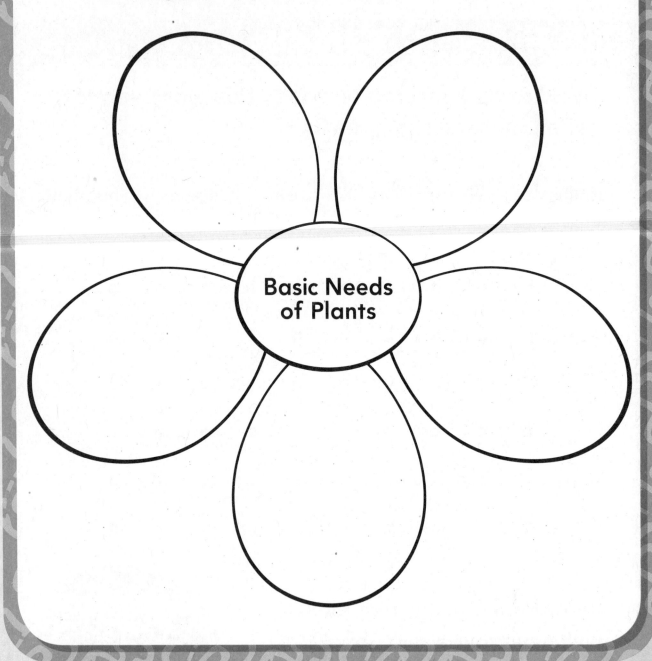

Basic Needs of Plants

Take It Home!

Family Members: With your child, talk about the plants that grow in or around your home. Ask your child to tell how the plants get the things they need to grow.

SC.2.L.17.1 Compare and contrast the basic needs that all living things, including humans, have for survival.

Lesson 2

Essential Question

What Are Animal Needs?

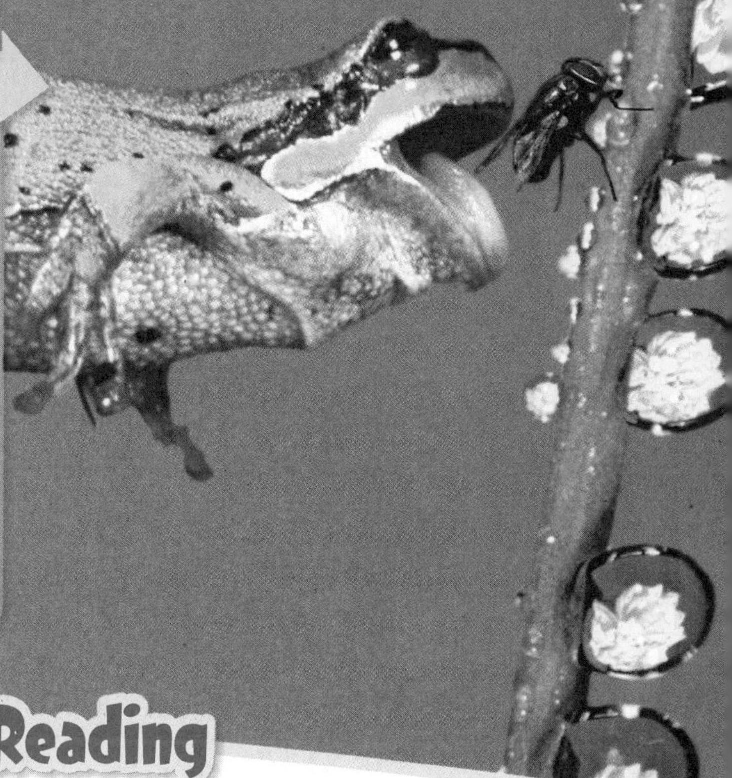

Engage Your Brain!

Find the answer to the question in the lesson.

How is a frog like a human?

Both need food

to ______________.

Active Reading

Lesson Vocabulary

1. Preview the lesson.
2. Write the 4 vocabulary terms here.

______________ ______________

______________ ______________

Just the Basics

Animals are living things. Humans are living things, too. Just like plants, animals and humans have basic needs. They must meet their basic needs in order to **survive**, or stay alive.

What basic need are these animals getting? How does this make animals like plants?

Active Reading

Circle the words that help you know what **survive** means.

Animals need water to survive.

Water Everywhere

Humans need water, too. Drinking water helps us survive. Water is also in other things we drink, such as milk and juice.

The water in this drink helps the girl get what she needs.

▶ Draw and label a picture to show what you like to drink.

Oranch

It's in the Air!

Living things need oxygen to survive. Humans and many animals use body parts called **lungs** to get oxygen from the air. Humans and these animals take in the air through their mouths and noses.

Put a hand on your chest and take a deep breath. Can you feel your lungs taking in air?

This boy is swimming underwater. He is using a snorkel.

▶ Why do people need a snorkel to swim underwater?

_____

_____

It's in the Water!

Some animals, such as fish, use gills to take in oxygen. **Gills** are parts of an animal that take in oxygen from the water. Can you find the gill on the side of the fish's head?

▶ Label the part of the fish that takes in oxygen.

_____

Do the Math!
Interpret a Table

Animal Breathing Rates

Use the chart to answer the questions.

Animal Name	Breaths per Minute
cat	25
dog	20
sparrow	50
horse	15

1. How many more breaths per minute does a sparrow take than a cat?

_____

2. How many more breaths per minute does a dog take than a horse?

_____

Food for Thought

Food is an important need for animals and humans. Food helps animals and humans grow and change. Some animals eat plants. Some eat other animals. Other animals and humans may eat both plants and animals.

A giraffe eats the leaves from trees.

▶ Draw a food you like to eat.

Protection for All

Animals need space to move, find food, and grow. Humans and many animals also need shelter. A **shelter** is a safe place to live.

Humans also need something that animals do not need. We need clothes to protect our bodies from cold and rainy weather.

Kinds of Shelters

Some bears live in dens.

Some bees live in hives.

A prairie dog lives in a burrow.

Some humans live in houses.

Active Reading

Circle the words that name different shelters.

Sum It Up!

① Circle It!

Circle the living thing that does **not** use lungs to get oxygen.

② Mark It!

Cross out the thing that humans do **not** need to survive.

③ Draw It!

Draw an animal in its shelter.
Show the animal meeting another need.

Name _____

Word Play

Read the words and the clues.
Write the word that goes with each clue.

| lungs | gills | shelter | survive | oxygen |

1 I am a safe place to live. ___ ___ ___ ___ ___ ___ ___

2 We are the body parts that you use to take in oxygen.

___ ___ ___ ___ ___

3 I mean to stay alive. ___ ___ ___ ___ ___ ___ ___

4 We are the body parts that fish and tadpoles use to stay alive in water.

___ ___ ___ ___ ___

5 I am in the air you breathe. ___ ___ ___ ___ ___ ___

Apply Concepts

Complete the Venn diagram. Show how animal needs and plant needs are alike and different.

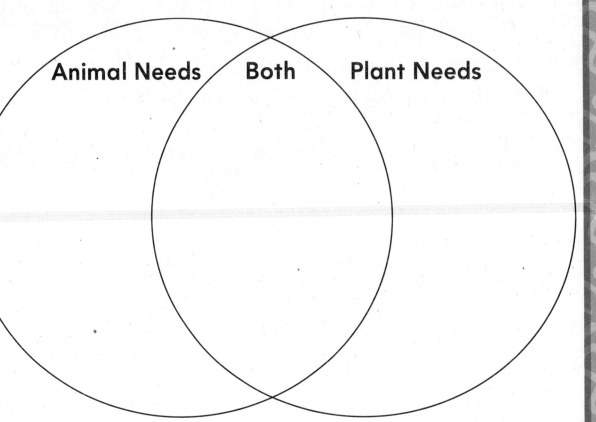

Animal Needs   Both   Plant Needs

Complete the sentence.
Tell about the main idea of this lesson.

Basic needs are the things that animals and plants

need to _____.

Take It Home!

Family Members: Talk about animals that you and your child have or know. Ask your child to tell how those animals meet their basic needs.

Name _____

SC.2.N.1.1 Raise questions . . . investigate them in teams . . . and generate appropriate explanations based on those explorations. **SC.2.N.1.3** Ask "how do you know?" in appropriate situations . . . . **SC.2.N.1.4** Explain how . . . scientific investigations should yield similar conclusions . . . . **SC.2.N.1.5** Distinguish between empirical observation . . . and ideas or inferences . . . . **SC.2.L.17.2** Recognize . . . living things are found all over Earth . . . live in habitats that meet its basic needs.

Essential Question

Can Plants Survive in Different Environments?

Set a Purpose

Write what you want to find out.

_____

Make a Prediction

Write a prediction about what you think will happen.

_____

_____

Think About the Procedure

❶ Why will you water the **desert** plant only once?

_____

❷ Why will you water the **rain forest** plant three times a day?

_____

263

Record Your Data

In this chart, record what you observe.

Date	Desert Plant	Rain Forest Plant

Draw Conclusions

Was your prediction right? Can a plant from one environment live in a different environment? How do you know?

_____

_____

Ask More Questions

What other questions could you ask about plants in different environments?

_____

_____

SC.2.L.17.2 Recognize and explain that living things are found all over Earth, but each is only able to live in habitats that meet its basic needs.

Lesson **4**

Essential Question

Where Do Plants and Animals Live?

Engage Your Brain!

Find the answer to the question in the lesson.

What kind of environment does this fish live in?

It lives in the

_____ .

Active Reading

Lesson Vocabulary

1 Preview the lesson.

2 Write the 2 vocabulary terms here.

_____ _____

265

All Around You

Look around you. All the living and nonliving things you see make up your **environment**. Living things from one environment usually cannot live in a different one. They live in the environment that meets their needs.

A **habitat** is a smaller part of an environment. A habitat is the place where a living thing gets the food, water, and shelter it needs.

Active Reading

Circle the words that tell what a **habitat** is.

Some fox kits live in a forest environment.

Salty Water

An ocean environment is a large body of salt water. The top layer of the ocean has the most living things. Here, plants get the sunlight they need, and animals find food. There is no sunlight in the deepest parts of the ocean.

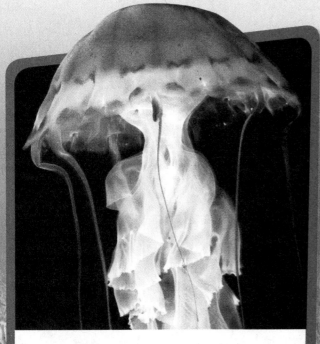

A jellyfish's tentacles sting and catch its food.

Kelp makes its own food. Many animals eat it.

▶ Why do plants live near the top layer of the ocean?

_____

_____

In a Rain Forest

A rain forest gets a lot of rain. The trees grow tall and block the sun. The plants on the forest floor do not need much sunlight. Animals, such as monkeys and birds, can use the tall trees as habitats.

These living things can live in the rain forest because it meets their needs.

▶ Draw a rain forest animal that might live in the trees.

Dry As a Bone

A desert environment is very dry and gets little rain. Desert plants store water in their thick stems or leaves. In hot deserts, many animals hide during the day.

A Joshua tree can be a habitat for birds, insects, and small animals.

Desert plants and animals can survive with little water.

desert hare

Gila monster

▶ Draw a cactus.

cactus

It's Cold Out Here!

A tundra environment is a very cold and snowy place. Plants and shrubs grow close together and low to the ground. Animals have thick fur that helps keep them warm.

An Arctic fox's white fur is hard to see against the snow.

purple saxifrage flowers

▶ How does an Arctic fox's white fur help it in winter?

_____

_____

On the Prairie

Tall grasses and wildflowers live in a prairie environment. A prairie is mostly dry with just a few kinds of trees or shrubs. Large animals eat the grasses. Smaller animals and insects find habitats among the grasses.

Active Reading

Read the labels. Circle the name of the animal that finds food and shelter in prairie grasses.

Bison travel in herds and eat prairie grasses.

coneflowers

prairie dogs

red-tailed hawk

Sum It Up!

1 Draw It!

Choose an environment. Draw the living and nonliving things in that environment.

2 Label It!

Name the environment in which you would find each living thing.

_____ _____ _____

Name _____

Word Play

Use the words below to complete the puzzle.

habitat	desert	environment
rain forest	tundra	prairie

Across

❶ a cold, snowy environment

❷ a dry, grassy environment

❸ a dry environment

Down

❹ all the living and nonliving things in a place

❺ an environment with tall trees and lots of rain

❻ a place where a living thing has the food, water, and shelter it needs to live

Apply Concepts

Write two details that go with the main idea. One detail should be about animals in that environment. The other should be about plants in that environment. Then answer the question.

Main Idea
A tundra is a cold, snowy environment.

Detail	Detail
_____ _____ _____	_____ _____ _____

What do all the living and nonliving things in a place make up? _____

© Houghton Mifflin Harcourt Publishing Company

Ask an Environmental Scientist

What do environmental scientists do?

We study the harmful effects to different kinds of environments.

How do environmental scientists help wildlife?

We find problems that affect wildlife and people in the environments. We figure out ways to solve those problems.

Sometimes people can harm an environment. For example, a factory may put waste into a stream. This may kill fish. We help the factory find other ways to get rid of its waste.

Now It's Your Turn!

▶ What question would you ask an environmental scientist?

_____

_____

_____

Making Environments Better

▶ Draw or write the answer to each question.

1 What do you think is most interesting about what environmental scientists do?

2 What might be difficult about what they do?

3 Why are environmental scientists important?

4 Think about being an environmental scientist. Draw an environment you would like to study.

1

2

3

4

Name _____

Multiple Choice

Fill in the circle next to the best answer.

SC.2.L.17.1

1 Look at the picture.

Tasha has two plants. She waters Plant A every day. She does not water Plant C. What will happen to Plant C?

Ⓐ Plant C will die.

Ⓑ Plant C will grow faster than Plant A.

Ⓒ Plant C will grow larger than Plant A.

SC.2.L.17.1

2 How are the needs of plants and animals alike?

Ⓐ Animals and plants both need sunlight to make their own food.

Ⓑ Animals and plants both need air and water to survive.

Ⓒ Animals and plants both need lungs to breathe.

SC.2.L.17.1

3 How is the animal using the tree in this picture?

Ⓐ It is using it for food.

Ⓑ It is using it for water.

Ⓒ It is using it for shelter.

SC.2.L.17.2

4 Why can't an Arctic fox live in a prairie dog's environment?

(A) The environment is far away.

(B) The environment is too wet.

(C) The environment does not meet its needs.

SC.2.N.1.5, SC.2.L.17.2

6 What can you infer by looking at this environment?

(A) The environment is very wet.

(B) The environment is very dry.

(C) The environment has many trees.

SC.2.N.1.1, SC.2.N.1.4, SC.2.L.17.2

5 You do a test that shows rain forest plants need water to live. How can you check that your results were correct?

(A) You can do the test again using desert plants.

(B) You can do the test again the same way.

(C) You can do the test in a different environment.

Interactive Glossary

This Interactive Glossary will help you learn how to spell and pronounce a vocabulary term. The Glossary will give you the meaning of the term. It will also show you a picture to help you understand what the term means.

Where you see **Your Turn** write your own words or draw your own picture to help you remember what the term means.

Glossary Pronunciation Key

With every glossary term, there is also a phonetic respelling. A phonetic respelling writes the word the way it sounds. This can help you pronounce new words. Use this key to help you understand the respellings.

Sound	As in	Phonetic Respelling	Sound	As in	Phonetic Respelling
a	bat	(BAT)	oh	over	(OH•ver)
ah	lock	(LAHK)	oo	pool	(POOL)
air	rare	(RAIR)	ow	out	(OWT)
ar	argue	(AR•gyoo)	oy	foil	(FOYL)
aw	law	(LAW)	s	cell	(SEL)
ay	face	(FAYS)		sit	(SIT)
ch	chapel	(CHAP•uhl)	sh	sheep	(SHEEP)
e	test	(TEST)	th	that	(THAT)
	metric	(MEH•trik)		thin	(THIN)
ee	eat	(EET)	u	pull	(PUL)
	feet	(FEET)	uh	medal	(MED•uhl)
	ski	(SKEE)		talent	(TAL•uhnt)
er	paper	(PAY•per)		pencil	(PEN•suhl)
	fern	(FERN)		onion	(UHN•yuhn)
eye	idea	(eye•DEE•uh)		playful	(PLAY•fuhl)
i	bit	(BIT)		dull	(DUHL)
ing	going	(GOH•ing)	y	yes	(YES)
k	card	(KARD)		ripe	(RYP)
	kite	(KYT)	z	bags	(BAGZ)
ngk	bank	(BANGK)	zh	treasure	(TREZH•er)

Interactive Glossary

A

attract [uh·TRAKT]
To pull toward something.
(p. 179)

B

basic needs [BAY·sik NEEDZ]
Certain things, such as food, water, air, and shelter, that a living thing needs to survive. (p. 246)

brain [BRAYN]
A part of the body that tells other parts of the body what to do. (p. 194)

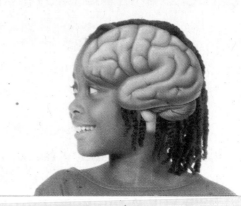

Your Turn

burning [BER·ning]
The changing of a substance into ashes and smoke. (p. 132)

C

clay [KLAY]

Soil that is sticky when wet and smooth when dry. It holds water well, but many kinds of plants don't grow well in it. (p. 57)

communicate [kuh·MYOO·ni·kayt]

To write, draw, or speak to show what you have learned. (p. 29)

condense [kuhn·DENS]

To change from a gas into tiny drops of water. (p. 73)

cone [KOHN]

A part of a pine tree and some other plants where seeds form. (p. 236)

D

dissolve [di·ZOLV]

To completely mix a solid with a liquid. (p. 130)

Interactive Glossary

draw conclusions
[DRAW kuhn·KLOO·zhuhnz]
To use information gathered during an investigation to see whether the results support the hypothesis. (p. 29)

energy [EN·er·jee]
Something that can cause matter to move or change. (p. 146)

E

electricity
[uh·lek·TRIH·sih·tee]
A form of energy. People produce electricity by using energy from other sources. (p. 147)

environment
[en·vy·ruhn·muhnt]
All the living and nonliving things in a place. (p. 266)

Your Turn

evaporate [ee·VAP·uh·rayt]
To change from a liquid into a gas. (p. 72)

freeze [FREEZ]
To change from a liquid to a solid. (p. 128)

Your Turn

F

force [FAWRS]
A push or a pull. (p. 164)

friction [FRIK·shuhn]
A force that slows or stops things that are touching. Friction also causes objects to get warmer when they rub together. (p. 169)

Interactive Glossary

G

gas [GAS]
A state of matter that fills all the space of its container. (p. 113)

germinate [JER·muh·nayt]
To start to grow. (p. 232)

gills [GILZ]
The parts of some animals that take in oxygen from the water. (p. 257)

gravity [GRAV·ih·tee]
A force that pulls all things toward the center of Earth. (p. 168)

H

habitat [HAB·ih·tat]
The place where a living thing finds food, water, and shelter. (p. 266)

Your Turn

heart [HAHRT]

A muscle that pumps blood throughout the body. (p. 199)

humus [HYOO·**muhs**]

Soil made of once-living things. (p. 57)

Your Turn

heat [HEET]

A kind of energy that makes things warmer. (p. 147)

hurricane [HER·**ih·kayn**]

A large storm with heavy rain and strong winds. (p. 85)

Interactive Glossary

hypothesis [hy·PAHTH·uh·sis]
A statement that you can test. (p. 27)

investigate [in·VES·tuh·gayt]
To plan and do a test to answer a question or solve a problem. (p. 26)

I

Your Turn

inquiry skills
[IN·kwer·ee SKILZ]
The skills people use to find out information. (p. 4)

L

larva
[LAHR·vuh]
Another name for a caterpillar. (p. 221)

life cycle [LYF SY·kuhl]
Changes that happen to an animal or a plant during its life. (p. 215)

lightning [LYT·ning]
A flash of electricity in the sky. (p. 84)

Your Turn

light [LYT]
A kind of energy that lets us see. (p. 147)

liquid [LIK·wid]
A state of matter that takes the shape of its container. (p. 112)

Interactive Glossary

lungs [LUHNGZ]

The parts of some animals that help them breathe by taking in oxygen from the air. (pp. 198, 256)

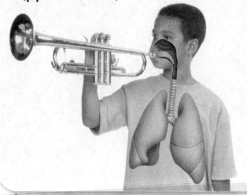

matter [MAT·er]

Anything that takes up space. (p. 98)

Your Turn

M

magnet [MAG·nit]

An object that can pull things made of iron or steel and can push or pull other magnets. (p. 178)

mass [MAS]

The amount of matter in an object. (p. 110)

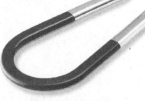

measure [MEZH·er]

To find the size, weight, or amount of something. (p. 100)

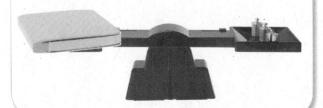

melt [MELT]

To change from a solid to a liquid. (p. 128)

muscles [MUHS·uhlz]

Body parts that help hold you up and work with bones to help you move. (p. 197)

Your Turn

metamorphosis [met·uh·MAWR·fuh·sis]

A series of changes in appearance that some animals go through. (p. 217)

N

nutrients [NOO·tree·uhnts]

Substances that help plants grow. (p. 249)

motion [MOH·shuhn]

When something is moving. Things are in motion when they move. (p. 164)

Interactive Glossary

pole [POHL]
A place on a magnet where the pull is the greatest. (p. 178)

precipitation
[pri·sip·uh·TAY·shuhn]
Water that falls from the sky. Rain, snow, sleet, and hail are kinds of precipitation. (p. 70)

property [PRAH·per·tee]
One part of what something is like. Color, size, and shape are each a property. (p. 98)

pupa [PYOO·puh]
The part of a life cycle when a caterpillar changes into a butterfly. (p. 221)

repel [rih·PEL]
To push away from something. (p. 179)

Your Turn

reproduce [ree·pruh·DOOS]
To have young, or more living things of the same kind. (p. 214)

S

sand [SAND]
Tiny pieces of rock. (p. 57)

science tools [SY·uhns TOOLZ]
The tools people use to find out information. (p. 14)

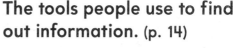

rock [RAHK]
A hard, nonliving object from the ground. (p. 42)

Your Turn

Interactive Glossary

seed [SEED]
The part of a plant that new plants grow from. (p. 230)

Your Turn

shelter [SHEL·ter]
A safe place to live. (p. 259)

skeleton [SKEL·uh·tuhn]
The bones that support your body and give it shape. (p. 196)

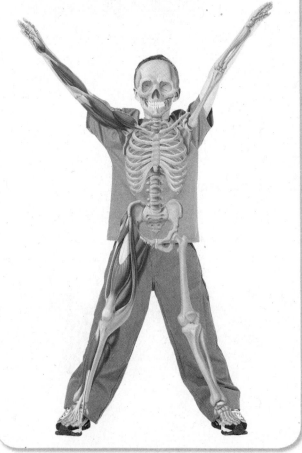

seedling [SEED·ling]
A young plant. (p. 233)

soil [SOYL]
Small pieces of rock and once-living things. (p. 54)

solid [SAHL·id]
The only state of matter that has its own shape. (p. 111)

Your Turn

solar energy [SOH·ler· EN·er·jee]
Energy from the sun. (p. 147)

speed [SPEED]
The measure of how fast something moves. (p. 166)

R15

Interactive Glossary

stomach [STUHM·uhk]

A baglike organ in the body that helps digest food. (p. 195)

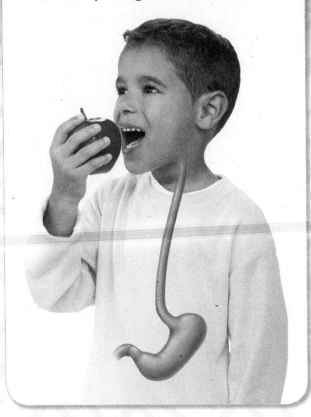

survive [ser·VYV]

To stay alive. (p. 254)

tadpole [TAD·pohl]

A young frog that comes out of an egg and has gills to take in oxygen from the water. (p. 216)

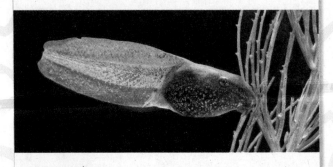

Your Turn

temperature [TEM·per·uh·cher]

A measure of how hot or cold something is. You can measure temperature with a thermometer. (p. 70)

texture [TEKS·cher]
The way something feels.
(p. 99)

thunderstorm
[THUHN·der·stawrm]
A storm with a lot of rain,
thunder, and lightning. (p. 84)

thermometer
[ther·MAHM·uh·ter]
A tool used to measure
temperature. (p. 15)

Your Turn

tornado [tawr·NAY·doh]
A spinning cloud with a cone
shape. (p. 85)

Interactive Glossary

W

water cycle
[WAW·ter SY·kuhl]
The movement of water from Earth to the air and back again. (p. 72)

Your Turn

water vapor
[WAW·ter VAY·per]
Water in the form of a gas. (p. 114)

weather [WEH·ther]
What the air outside is like. (p. 68)

weathering [WEH·ther·ing]
A kind of change that happens when wind and water break down rock into smaller pieces. (p. 43)

weight [WAYT]
A measure of how heavy something feels. (p. 101)

Index

Index

Keys, Fort Jefferson, 39
Miami, 143
oranges, 125
sea turtles, 211
surfing in, 191
swimming in, 95
water activities, 161
Flower, 3, 234, 239
dandelion, 229
and pinecones, 238
Food
for animals, 257, 262
for people, 257
Force, 163–165
cause and effect, 172
changing direction, 166–167
changing speed, 166–167
draw conclusions, 174
friction, 169, 171–172
gravity, 168, 170–172
pull, 164–165, 170, 172
push, 164–165, 170, 172
record data, 174
Fort Jefferson, Florida Keys, 39
Fort Myers, Thomas Edison's lab, 1
Freeze, 127–128, 135–136
Friction, 169, 171–172
Frog, 213, 222, 253
life cycle of, 216–217
metamorphosis, 217

Gas, 109–110, 113–114, 116, 118. *See also* **Liquid**
Geologist, 51. *See also* **Scientists**
Germinate, seed, 232
Gills, 257, 261
Gravity, 163, 168, 170–172

H

Habitat, 266, 268–269, 273
Hand lens, 14, 18–20. *See also* **Science tools**
Heart, 199, 203. *See also* **Body parts**
blood, 199
comparison to other muscles, 199
effect of exercise on, 200, 202
functions, 199
healthy, 200
Heart rate
change of, 207–208
draw conclusions, 208
record data, 208
Heat, 147, 152–153. *See also* **Energy**
Humus, 56–59
Hurricane, 85, 89. *See also* **Weather**
Florida, 65

Hypothesis, 27, 32–34

Ice
freeze and cut, 127
on plants, 67
Infer, 9–11
Inquiry Skills, 4
classify, 7, 10, 12
compare, 7, 11–12, 50, 107–108, 121, 227
communicate, 29, 32–34
draw conclusions, 24, 29, 32–34, 36, 62, 80, 82, 108, 122, 138, 156, 174, 188, 208, 228, 264
hypothesize, 79, 81, 121, 155, 173, 187, 207
infer, 9–11
make a model, 8, 12, 36
measure, 6, 10–12, 15–18, 21, 31, 66, 71, 75, 94, 107–108, 155
observe, 4–5, 7, 9–11, 14, 23, 26, 32–34, 62, 80, 82, 174, 208, 228, 264
order, 7, 32, 58, 76, 104–105, 107–108, 226
plan investigation, 5, 10, 12

Index

© Houghton Mifflin Harcourt Publishing Company

Index

Index